HEALTH SERVICES
MANAGEMENT

A Book of Cases
Sixth Edition

Edited by Anthony R. Kovner
and Duncan Neuhauser

Health Administration Press, Chicago, Illinois
AUPHA Press, Washinton, D.C.

AUPHA
HAP

HEALTH SERVICES
MANAGEMENT

A Book of Cases
Sixth Edition

05 04 03 02 01   5 4 3 2 1

Library of Congress Cataloging-in-Publication Data

Health services management : a book of cases / edited by Anthony R.
Kovner and Duncan Neuhauser. — 6th ed.
    p.   cm.
  Includes bibliographical references and index.
  ISBN 1-56793-146-4 (alk. paper)
    1. Health facilities—Administration—Case studies.   2. Health
services administration—Case studies.   3. Hospitals—
Administration—Case studies.   I. Kovner, Anthony R.   II. Neuhauser,
Duncan, 1939–
  RA971 .H43   2000
  362.1'068—dc21   00–059694

The paper used in this publication meets the minimum requirements of American National Standard for Information Sciences—Permanence of Paper for Printed Library Materials, ANSI Z39.48–1984. ⊚™

Health Administration Press
A division of the Foundation
  of the American College of
  Healthcare Executives
One North Franklin Street
Suite 1700
Chicago, Illinois 60606
(312) 424-2800

Association of University Programs
  in Health Administration
1911 North Fort Myer Drive, Suite 503
Arlington, Virginia 22209
(703) 524-5500

Contents

Part III   Organizational Design

Part IV   Professional Integration

Part V   Adaptation

Part VI   Accountability

Preface to the Sixth Edition

This book was developed as a complementary text to our book, *Health Services Management: Readings and Commentary*, first published in 1978, and in its seventh edition in 2001. We are delighted, in response to user demand and a need to keep more of the cases current, to prepare this sixth edition of our casebook.

We use the same organizing framework as in the book of readings: the role of the health manager, control, organization design, clinician integration, adaptation, and accountability. The casebook can stand on its own, however, in teaching students and managers through the case method approach.

This edition contains many new cases and several that appeared in previous editions, but have been updated.

All of these cases have been tested in the classroom. They have been selected because they take place in a variety of settings and are written from the perspective of managers who must define and respond to particular complex situations.

Anthony R. Kovner
Duncan Neuhauser

Learning Through the Case Method

Anthony R. Kovner

A challenge for many graduate programs in health services management is bridging the gap between theory and skills and their application by students to health services organizations. Part of the problem lies in the difficulty of attracting and retaining skilled teachers who can integrate perspectives and apply concepts across disciplines in responding to managerial problems and opportunities.

A second challenge is to prepare graduate students to communicate effectively, in writing and orally, and to assist them in working effectively in groups. This includes helping students to assess the effects of their personalities or behavioral styles on others—are they perceived as abrasive, wishy-washy, manipulative? Are they aware of how others interpret not only their words but tone and body language?

Students in graduate programs of health services management need to understand their own values and those of others who differ in educational background, political and religious orientation, clinical experience, or familial exposure to careers and lifestyles.

A "case" is a description of a situation or problem facing a manager that requires analysis, decision, and planning a course of action. A decision may be to delay a decision, and a planned course of action may be to take no action. A case takes place in time. A case must have an issue. As McNair says: "There must be a question of what should somebody do, what should somebody have done, who is to blame for the situation, what is the best decision to be made under the circumstances."[1] A case represents selected details about a situation; it represents selection by the casewriter.

The case method involves class discussion that is guided by a teacher so that students can diagnose and define important problems in a situation, acquire competence in developing useful alternatives to respond to such problems, and improve judgment in selecting action alternatives. Students learn ways both to diagnose constraints and opportunities faced by the manager in implementation and to overcome constraints given limited time and dollars.

Teachers can transmit great quantities of data to students more effectively and certainly more efficiently by lecture. The teacher is assumed to be correct in presenting facts, and the student transcribes key points of the lecture and transmits them back to the teacher at examination time. In contrast, in a case course, the teacher's job is to engage the students in a management simulation so that they can think independently, communicate effectively, and defend their opinions logically with reference to underlying assumptions and values. Often a case does not have one right answer because at least two sides are present in the issue at hand.

Students often have difficulty adjusting to a classroom without an authority figure, without lectures from which to take notes, and in which little information is offered by the teacher, at least until the class discussion has ended. Some students find it irritating to have to listen to their peers when they are paying to learn what the teacher has to say.

In a case course, students learn how to use information at the point of decision. Many students dislike "putting themselves on the line" when they are "only" students saying what they think. If no "right" answers can be reached, students quickly learn in a case course that many "wrong" answers can be eliminated because of faulty logic or assumptions that are challenged or contradicted by their peers. Students fear looking foolish and being downgraded accordingly by the teacher, and they must pass the course,[2] but students should consider such self-exposure to be little enough cost to pay in relation to the benefit of appearing mature and skillful after graduation and in the professional environment. It is hoped that they will have gained the ability to make logical judgments and learned how to behave and communicate their opinions to others.

As Cantor[3] says, "You don't learn from anybody else's experience or from your own experience unless you go through the experience to learn." This is what the case method has to offer students—an experience in learning that involves testing opinions and conclusions against the reality of the case and the judgment of peers and teacher.

How do cases bridge the gap between theory and skills and their application by managers? Problems that health services managers face do not come neatly packaged as separate questions of statistics, economics, organization theory, or policy analysis. Rather they are organizational, multidisciplinary problems, sometimes difficult to define as well as to resolve. Problems may include negotiating a new contract with the chief of radiology, responding appropriately to patient complaints, or taking responsibility for quality assurance in relation to a surgeon's poor performance.

Student performance in a case course is typically assessed on class participation and on written analysis of case materials. A lack of sufficient time by the teacher in analyzing a student's evaluation may be partially corrected by allowing peer evaluation as well. Often teachers ask students to collaborate on complex cases or to evaluate each other's performance. The presenting student should be told if personal style or mannerisms interfere with a case analysis presentation or with its perception by others, as these issues could create conflicts in their professional careers.

In a case course, students are often asked to adopt the perspectives of certain characters in the case, to play certain roles. To deny someone of something or to persuade someone to do something requires an understanding of that person's needs and perceptions of the decision maker. Role-playing can promote a better understanding of viewpoints that otherwise may seem irrational given a student's prior understanding of what should be done in a particular situation. Students can better understand their own values and underlying assumptions when their opinions are challenged by peers and teachers.

To conclude, it is important to understand what a case is not and what case method cannot teach. Cases are not real life—they present only part of a situation. Writing or communicating a case may be as difficult as or more difficult than evaluating someone else's written case. Like many a consultant, the student can never see the results—what would have happened if the case participants had followed his advice.

Some aspects of management can be learned only by managing. How else can one understand when someone says one thing but means another? How else can one judge whether to confront or oppose a member of the ruling coalition when that member's behavior appears to threaten the long-range interests of the organization? Students and managers have to form and adopt their own value systems and make their own decisions. A case course can give students a better understanding of the nature of the role they will be playing as managers—an understanding that can help them to manage better, if not well.

Notes

1.   Andrew R. Towl, *To Study Administration by Cases* (Boston: Graduate School of Business Administration, Harvard University, 1969), p. 67.

2.   Ibid., p. 68.

3.   Ibid., p. 155.

A Short History of the Case Method of Teaching

Karen Schachter Weingrod
Duncan Neuhauser

Teaching by example is no doubt as old as the first parent and child. In medicine it surely started with a healer, the first apprentice, and a patient. The ancient Greeks codified medical principles, rules, and laws. University education in medicine started about 800 years ago, focused on abstract principles and scholastic reasoning, and was removed from practicality. By 1750 in England, the professions aspired to gentlemen status.[1] The goldheaded cane of the English physician, for instance, was the clear symbol that his hands were not expected to touch patients, unlike the hands of apothecaries and barber surgeons. Later, the American sociologist Thorstein Veblen, in *The Theory of the Leisure Class*, used the example of the cane as symbolic that a gentleman need not work with his hands.[2] In the late 1700s in France, medical education moved into hospitals or "the clinic," where patients in large numbers could be observed, autopsies performed, and the physiological state linked back to the patients' signs and symptoms.[3] This was one step in the departure from the abstract medical theorizing in universities (often about the "four humours"), which may have had no bearing on actual disease processes.

Education in law also became increasingly abstract, conveyed through the erudite lecture. It built theoretical constructs and was logically well reasoned. The professor spoke and the student memorized and recited without much opportunity for practical experience or discussion. This had become the standard by the late 1850s.

It is only by comparison with what went on before in universities that the case method of teaching represented such a striking change.

The historical development of the case method can be traced to Harvard University. Perhaps it is not surprising that this change occurred in the United States rather than in Europe, with the American inclinations toward democratic equality, practicality, and positivism, and the lack of interest in classic abstract theorizing.

The change started in 1870 when the president of Harvard University, Charles William Eliot, appointed the obscure lawyer Christopher Columbus Langdell to be dean of the Harvard Law School.

Langdell believed law to be a science. In his own words: "Law considered as a science, consists of certain principles or doctrines. To have such a mastery of these as to be able to apply them with constant faculty and certainty to the ever-tangled skein of human affairs, is what constitutes a good lawyer; and hence to acquire that mastery should be the business of every earnest student of the law."[4]

The specimens needed for the study of Langdell's science of law were judicial opinions as recorded in books and stored in libraries. He accepted the science of law, but he turned the learning process back to front. Instead of giving a lecture that would define a principle of law and give supporting examples of judicial opinions, he gave the students the judicial opinions without the principle and by use of a Socratic dialogue extracted from the students in the classroom the principles that would make sense out of the cases. The student role was now active rather than passive. Students were subjected to rigorous questioning of the case material. They were asked to defend their judgments and to confess to error when their judgments were illogical. Although this dialectic was carried on by the professor and one or two students at a time, all of the students learned and were on the edge of their seats, fearing or hoping they would be called on next. The law school style that evolved has put the student under public pressure to reason quickly, clearly, and coherently in a way that is valuable in the courtroom or during negotiation. After a discouraging start, Langdell attracted such able instructors as Oliver Wendell Holmes, Jr. They carried the day, and now the case method of teaching is nearly universal in American law schools.

The introduction of the case method of teaching to medicine is also known. A Harvard medical student of the class of 1901, Walter B. Cannon, shared a room with Harry Bigelow, a third-year law student.

The excitement with which Bigelow and his classmates debated the issues within the cases they were reading for class contrasted sharply with the passivity of medical school lectures.

In 1900, discussing the value of the case method in medicine, Harvard President Charles Eliot described the earlier medical education as follows:

> I think it was thirty-five years ago that I was a lecturer at the Harvard Medical School for one winter; at that time lectures began in the school at eight o'clock in the morning and went on steadily till two o'clock—six mortal hours, one after the other of lectures, without a question from the professor, without the possibility of an observation by the student, none whatever, just the lecture to be listened to, and possibly taken notes of. Some of the students could hardly write.[5]

In December 1899, Cannon persuaded one of his instructors, G. L. Walton, to present one of the cases in written form from his private practice as an experiment. Walton printed a sheet with the patient's history and allowed the students a week to study it. The lively discussion that ensued in class made Walton an immediate convert.[6] Other faculty soon followed, including Richard C. Cabot.

Through the case method, medical students would learn to judge and interpret clinical data, to estimate the value of evidence, and to recognize the gaps in their knowledge—something that straight lecturing could never reveal. The case method of teaching allowed students to throw off passivity in the lecture hall and integrate their knowledge of anatomy, physiology, pathology, and therapeutics into a unified mode of thought.

As a student, Cannon wrote two articles about the case method in 1900 for the *Boston Medical and Surgical Journal* (later to become *The New England Journal of Medicine*).[7] He sent a copy of one of these papers to the famous clinician professor Dr. William Osler of Johns Hopkins University. Osler replied, "I have long held that the only possible way of teaching students the subject of medicine is by personal daily contact with cases, which they study not only once or twice, but follow systematically."[8] If a written medical case was interesting, a real live patient in the classroom could be memorable. Osler regularly introduced patients to his class, asked students to interview and examine the patient and discuss the medical problems involved. He would regularly send students to the library and laboratory to seek answers and report back to the rest of the class.[9] This is ideal teaching.

Osler's students worshipped him, but with today's division of labor in medicine between basic science and clinical medicine, such a synthesis is close to impossible.

The May 24, 1900 issue of the *Boston Medical and Surgical Journal* was devoted to articles and comments by Eliot, Cannon, Cabot, and others about the case method of teaching. In some ways this journal issue remains the best general discussion of the case method. This approach was adopted rapidly at other medical schools, and books of written cases quickly followed in neurology (1902), surgery (1904), and orthopedic surgery (1905).[10]

Walter Cannon went on to a distinguished career in medical research. Richard C. Cabot joined the medical staff of the Massachusetts General Hospital, and in 1906 published his first book of cases. (He also introduced the first social worker into a hospital.[11]) He was concerned about the undesirable separation of clinical physicians and pathologists; too many diagnoses were turning out to be false at autopsy. To remedy this, Cabot began to hold his case exercises with students, house officers, and visitors.

Cabot's clinical/pathological conferences took on a stereotypical style and eventually were adopted in teaching hospitals throughout the world. First, the patient's history, symptoms, and test results would be described. Then an invited specialist would discuss the case, suggest an explanation, and give a diagnosis. Finally, the pathologist would present the autopsy or pathological diagnosis and questions would follow to elaborate points.

In 1915, Cabot sent written copies of his cases to interested physicians as "at home case method exercises." These became so popular that in 1923 the *Boston Medical and Surgical Journal* began to publish one per issue.[12] This journal has since changed its name to *The New England Journal of Medicine*, but the "Cabot Case Records" still appear with each issue.

A look at a current *New England Journal of Medicine* case will show how much the case method has changed since Christopher Columbus Langdell's original concept. The student or house officer is no longer asked to discuss the case; rather, it is the expert who puts her reputation on the line. She has the opportunity to demonstrate wisdom, but can also be refuted in front of a large audience. Although every physician in the audience probably makes mental diagnoses, the case presentation has become a passive affair, like a lecture.

Richard Cabot left the Massachusetts General Hospital to head the Social Relations (sociology, psychology, cultural anthropology) department at Harvard. He brought the case method with him, but it disappeared from use there by the time of his death in 1939.[13] The social science disciplines were concerned with theory building, hypothesis testing, and research methodology, and to such "unapplied" pure scientists perhaps the case method was considered primitive. Further, the use of the case method of teaching also diminished in the first two preclinical years of medical school as clinical scientists came more and more to the fore with their laboratory work and research on physiology, pharmacology, biochemistry, and molecular biology. Currently a return to a problem-solving focus in medical school is being advocated by a task force of the American Association of Medical Colleges.

In 1908, the Harvard Business School was created as a department of the Graduate School of Arts and Sciences. It was initially criticized as merely a school for "successful money-making." Early on an effort was made to teach through the use of written problems involving situations faced by actual business executives, presented in sufficient factual detail to enable students to develop their own decisions. The school's first book of cases, on marketing, was published in 1922 by Melvin T. Copeland.[14]

Today, nearly every class in the Harvard Business School is taught by the case method. In 1957, the Intercollegiate Case Clearing House was founded. Physically located on the Harvard campus, it housed approximately 40,000 cases and added 1,000 to 1,200 new cases each year. Cases were made available to other universities. Recently the clearing house was renamed HBS Case Services and now limits itself to cases produced at the Harvard Business School.

Unlike the law school, where cases come directly from judicial decisions (sometimes abbreviated by the instructor) and the medical school, where the patient is the basis for the case, the business faculty and their aides must enter organizations to collect and compile their material. This latter mode of selection offers substantial editorial latitude. Here more than elsewhere the case writer's vision, or lack of it, defines the content of the case.

Unlike a pathologist's autopsy diagnosis, a business case is not designed to have a right answer. In fact, one usually never knows whether the business in question lives or dies. Rather, the cases are written in a way that splits a large class (up to 80 students) into factions. The best cases are those that create divergent opinions; the professor becomes more an orchestra leader than a source of truth. The professor's opinion or answer may never be made explicit. Following a discussion, a student's question related to what really happened or what should have been done may be answered, "I don't know" or "I think the key issues were picked up in the case discussion." Such hesitancy on the part of the instructor is often desirable. To praise or condemn a particular faction in the classroom can discourage future discussions.

The class atmosphere in a business school is likely to be less pressured than in a law school. Like a good surgeon, a good lawyer must often think very quickly, but unlike the surgeon his thinking is demonstrated verbally and publicly. He must persuade by the power of his logic rather than by force of authority. Business and management are different. Key managerial decisions—What business are we in? Who are our customers? Where should we be ten years from now?—may take months or even years to answer.

The fact that the business manager's time frame reduces the pressure for immediate answers makes management education different from physician education in other ways. Physicians are required to absorb countless facts on anatomy, disease symptoms, and drug side effects. Confronted with 20 patients a day, the physician has no time to consult references and must rely on memory instead. The manager can look up information, given the longer time horizon of decision making in business. Therefore, managerial education focuses more on problem-solving techniques than on memorization of data.

Not all business schools have endorsed the case method of teaching. The University of Chicago Business School, for example, rarely uses cases and focuses on teaching the "science" of economics, human behavior, and operations research. The faculty are concerned with theory building, hypothesis testing, statistical methodology, and the social sciences. Stanford Business School uses about half social sciences and half case method. Each school is convinced that its teaching philosophy is best and believes others to be misguided. Conceptually, the debate can be broken into two aspects: science versus professionalism, and active versus passive learning.

There is little question that active student involvement in learning is better than passive listening to lectures. The case method is one of many approaches to increasing student participation. However, only a skilled instructor, for example, can stimulate a lively discussion by social sciences students on the theoretical assumptions, methodological problems, and use or abuse of statistical analysis in an *American Journal of Sociology* assignment.

Academic science is not overly concerned with the practical problems of the world, but professionals are and professional education should be. The lawyer, physician, and manager cannot wait for perfect knowledge; they have to make decisions "in the face of uncertainty." Science can help with these decisions to varying degrees. To the extent that scientific theories have the power to predict and explain, they can be used by professionals. In the jargon of statistics: the higher the percentage of variance explained, the more useful the scientific theory, the smaller the role for clinical or professional judgment, and the greater the role for case method teaching as opposed to, for example, mathematical problem solving.

It can be argued that the professional will always be working at the frontier of the limits of scientific prediction. When science is the perfect predictor, then often the problem is solved, or the application is delegated to computers or technicians, or, as in some branches of engineering, professional skills focus on the manipulation of accurate but complex mathematical equations.

Scientific medicine now understands smallpox so well that it no longer exists. Physicians spend most of their time on problems that are not solved: cancer, heart disease, or the common complaints of living that bring most people to doctors. In management, the budget cycle, personnel position control, sterile operating room environment, and maintenance of the business office ledgers are handled routinely by organizational members and usually do not consume the attention of the chief executive officer. In law, the known formulations become the "boiler plate" of contracts.

The debate between business schools over the use of cases illustrates the difference in belief in the power of the social sciences in the business environment. Teaching modes related to science and judgment will always be in uneasy balance with each other, shifting with time and place. A few innovative medical schools have moved away from the scientific lectures of the preclinical years and toward a case problem-solving mode (e.g., the University of Limburg in Maastricht, Holland). On the other side of the coin, a quiet revolution is being waged in clinical reasoning. The principles of statistics, epidemiology, and economics, filtered through the techniques of decision analysis, cost-effectiveness analysis, computer modeling, and artificial intelligence, are making the Cabot Case Record approach obsolete for clinical reasoning. Scientific methods of clinical reasoning are beginning to replace aspects of professional or clinical judgment in medicine.[15]

This does not mean that the professional aspect of medicine will be eliminated by computer-based science. Rather, the frontiers, the unknown areas calling for professional judgment, will shift to new areas, such as the development of socio-emotional rapport with patients—what used to be called "the bedside manner.[16]"

The cases that make up this book are derived from the business school style of case teaching. As such they do not have answers. The cases can be used to apply management concepts to practical problems; however, these concepts (scientific theory seems too strong a term to apply to them) may help solve these case problems but will not yield the "one right answer." They all leave much room for debate.

Notes

1.   Harold J. Cook, *The Decline of the Old Medical Regime in Stuart London* (Ithaca, NY: Cornell University Press, 1986).

2.   Thorstein Veblen, *The Theory of the Leisure Class* (1899; reprinted New York: Mentor, 1953).

3.   Michel Foucault, *The Birth of the Clinic* (New York: Vintage, 1973).

4.   C. C. Langdell, *Cases and Contracts* (1871), cited in *The Law at Harvard*, by Arthur E. Sutherland (Cambridge, MA: Harvard University Press, 1967), p. 174.

5.   Charles Eliot, "The Inductive Method Applied to Medicine," *Boston Medical and Surgical Journal* 142, no. 22 (24 May 1900): 557.

6.   Saul Benison, A. Clifford Barger, and Elin L. Wolfe, *Walter B. Cannon, The Life and Times of a Young Scientist* (Cambridge, MA: Harvard University Press, 1987), pp. 65–75, 417–418.

7.   W. B. Cannon, "The Case Method of Teaching Systematic Medicare," *Boston Medical and Surgical Journal* 142, no. 2 (11 January 1900): 31–36; and "The Case System in Medicine" 142, no. 22 (24 May 1900): 563–64.

8.   Benison et al., *Walter B. Cannon . . .* p. 66.

9.   Alan M. Chesney, *The Johns Hopkins Hospital and the Johns Hopkins University School of Medicine*, vol. 11, 1893–1905 (Baltimore, MD: The Johns Hopkins Press, 1958), pp. 125–28.

10.   Benison et al., *Walter B. Cannon . . .* p. 418.

11.   Although not the first hospital-based social worker to work with Cabot, his best-known social worker colleague was Walter Cannon's sister, Ida Cannon. Ibid., p. 145.

12.   These cases start October 25, 1923.

13.   Paul Buck (ed.), *The Social Sciences at Harvard* (Boston, MA: Harvard University Press, 1965).

14.   For more on the history of the case method of teaching managers see Roy Penchansky, *Health Services Administration: Policy Cases and the Case Method* (Boston, MA: Harvard University Press, 1968), pp. 395–453.

15.   Barnes, Louis B., Christensen, C. Roland, Hansen, Abby J. *Teaching and the Case Method,* 3rd Edition (Boston, MA, Harvard Business School Press, 1994).

16.   A proposal to increase the problem-solving content of medical education is found in Association of American Medical Colleges, *Graduate Medical Education: Proposals for the Eighties* (Washington, DC: AAMC, 1980). Also reprinted as a supplement in *Journal of Medical Education* 56, no. 9 (September 1981, part 2).

Part I

The Role of the Manager

Introduction

Personnel decisions, critical to managerial effectiveness, are often postponed by managers. Considerably more time may be spent on the decision to purchase or lease a piece of equipment costing $900,000 with a useful life of seven years than on the decision to hire a registered nurse earning $45,000 who may work for the organization for 20 years. Because managers are far outnumbered by other employees and staff, health services executives are often more careful in selecting their own subordinates or colleagues.

An important aspect of employing a manager is determining the time to spend on the search and the amount of funds to expend on advertising. Someone must decide who will screen candidates, who will check references, how many candidates should be interviewed, and who should see the job applicant.

Perhaps even more important than the hiring decision is the continuous evaluation and motivation of subordinates and colleagues, many of whom may have been hired by the manager's predecessors. If a manager is not performing at the level of competence her supervisor expects, what are the latter's options? What are the manager's options if she disagrees with her supervisor's expectations or evaluation? If the supervising manager does not fire or transfer the manager being evaluated, her own effectiveness may suffer because she lacks a key aide to implement her decisions or augment her politics. But this ineffective manager may have been working loyally in the organization for many years, and searching for and training a new manager carries costs; in addition, the risk exists that a new hire's behavior will not be as anticipated.

Managerial personnel decisions become even more complicated when, as in "the Associate Director and the Controllers," the health services manager is dealing with a functional specialist who is line-responsible to the top manager and staff-responsible to the chief controller in a multi-unit medical center. The straight and dotted lines of authority on the organizational chart become fuzzy and difficult to agree on, especially when the associate director's boss and the medical center director of finance distrust each other. In this selection, key staff of two recently merged units have different value orientations—the base hospital primarily serving attending physicians in their private practice and the ambulatory health services program emphasizing the provision of respectful patient care to the needy.

Management is often a lonely occupation and preoccupation. Important decisions are seldom made on an either-or basis and usually involve personal as well as organizational benefits and risks. In "A New Faculty Practice Administrator for the Department of Medicine," the weighing of risks and benefits is different for Sam Bones, the chief of medicine, than it is for Sandra Compson, the group practice administrator, or for Compson's eventual successor. Similarly, in "The Associate Director and the Controllers," the stakes of the game are higher for Jim Joel, the ambulatory health services program administrator, and for Percy Oram, its controller, than for Milton Schlitz, the medical center director of finance, and for Miller Harrang, the chief executive officer of the ambulatory health services program.

Why must Joel decide to do anything at all? In "A New Faculty Practice Administrator," Bones must choose a new group practice administrator. But in "The Associate Director and the Controllers," Joel can decide to not get involved and allow Harrang and Schlitz to deal with the consequences of Oram's ineffectiveness. How much should it matter to Joel whether Oram remains in the job or not, so long as Joel can protect his own job? On the other hand, Joel is being paid to manage, not to observe nor to protect himself. Good management generally makes a difference to the paying customer and, more important for the manager, to the ruling coalition of the organization. How much of a difference it makes is open to debate. But no one will look after the manager's interest if he will not look after it himself. This is a first rule of managerial self-preservation and of managerial system maintenance. Looking after oneself does not mean that the manager should lock the office door and read reports. Nor does it require offending those in the ruling coalition perceived to be acting against the long-term organizational interest. In a rare case, the manager may be better served in offending members of the ruling coalition. The costs of not offending them may also be great. But the manager should first weigh whether he is willing to pay the consequences of offending such members, in terms of his own authority and position.

Health services managers often face tremendous pressures from the government to move in a certain direction, and resistance from physicians, who are urging not one iota of movement further than that required by the letter of the law. If a strategic plan developed by consultants assumes increases of 20 percent in unduplicated patient count in the service area, the manager may be persuaded (or may persuade herself) to accept the assumption to assure board approval, although a 5 percent increase is more likely. The manager can always defend her decision, and the deficiency in her estimates may seem less important after the plan is accepted and new marketing staff has been hired.

How much value do managers add to organizational performance? Not much, according to Pfeffer and Salancik, who argue that the contribution of managers accounts for about 10 percent of the variance in organizational performance, and that "the sportscasters' cliche that managers are hired to be fired reflects a great amount of truth about all managers."[1] A great amount of evidence, however, indicates that managers *do* make a difference in organizational performance, if only because managers often play a principal role in obtaining resources for the organization, a function on which Pfeffer and Salancik place such high priority. In any event, the contribution of health services managers to organizational effectiveness is seen by most organizational stakeholders as increasingly important, and managerial rewards and risks have been increasing in recent years.

If the health services manager can never meet all the expectations of key stakeholders/participants in her organization, she can at least be perceived as taking their interests into account in policy formulation and implementation. Unfortunately, this involves regular communication with numerous participants, the time for which is not always available— although, perhaps, more available than most managers are willing to admit. We are assuming that key participants prefer to trust the manager (rather than get rid of her) based on her stated willingness to implement specified and agreed-upon organizational goals with which they may not personally agree.

What makes for an effective manager? The answer depends on who answers as well as on a given manager's actual actions or actions perceived by superiors, subordinates, and peers. Sometimes an effective manager—as in the case of "The Nowhere Job"—should consider resigning. Clearly, the health services manager must acquire certain information, possess certain skills, and have certain values consistent with the organizational context in which she functions. It is not always easy to decide what to do after the manager receives disquieting information such as that shown in the case of "Manager Morale of Uptown Hospital."

In assessing the four applicants for the position of group practice administrator or in evaluating Associate Director Joel's performance in the two cases in this section, ask yourself the following questions:

1. Do these managers have adequate knowledge of the power structure of their organizations and institutional environments, as well as an understanding of key participants who can affect their activities and responsibilities?
2. Do they possess the necessary interpersonal and analytical skills to function effectively?
3. Have they shown good judgment in making or in not making certain decisions?
4. Do they have personalities appropriate to their job situations and to the people with whom they are working?

Evaluating managerial effectiveness or contribution carries a cost. All pertinent information may not be available. Reliance on measuring managerial performance may divert attention inappropriately from the manager's overall performance to criteria that can be measured easily.

Ensuring financial flows to the health services organization is an important criterion for effective managerial performance. And yet, despite the importance of financial flows, considerable ambiguity exists about this criterion in Bones's faculty group practice, relative to the research and teaching goals of the department of medicine, and in Joel's health center, relative to providing free and respectful patient care to the indigent and sick. For the staff involved may feel that the financial flows will continue, regardless of the success of the group practice in attracting more patients or of whether the health center is succeeding in collecting more dollars from the indigent.

Evaluating managers, like management itself, involves judgment, which in Ray Brown's phrase is "knowledge ripened by experience."[2] We are hopeful that these cases can be useful in ripening student judgment and in clarifying for students the assumptions on which they will make future decisions.

Case Questions

A New Faculty Practice Administrator for the Department of Medicine

1. What criteria would you use in evaluating the four candidates?
2. What are the strengths and weaknesses of each candidate?
3. What are Bones's criteria in evaluating the four candidates?
4. Whom would you recommend to Bones as your selection for the position? Why?

The Associate Director and the Controllers

1. What is the problem from Joel's point of view? from Oram's point of view? from Harrang's and Schlitz's points of view?
2. In what ways should Oram be accountable to Joel and Schlitz?
3. Given that Oram's performance is not acceptable to Joel, what options does Joel have to affect Oram's performance?
4. What do you recommend that Joel do now? Why?
5. What are the constraints on effective implementation of your recommendations, and how might Joel overcome them?
6. What should Joel have done differently prior to the end point of the case that might have made the problem easier to solve now?
7. What conflict exists between the goals of Joel and Schlitz? In the face of such conflict, what are Oram's options in responding, and what would you recommend that Oram do now and why?

Notes

1. Jeffrey Pfeffer and Gerald R. Salancik, *The External Control of Organizations* (New York: Harper and Row, 1978), p. 17.

2. Ray Brown, *Judgment in Administration* (New York: McGraw-Hill, 1966), p. 9.

Selected Bibliography

Brown, Lawrence D. *Politics and Health Care Organization*. Washington, DC: The Brookings Institution, 1983, pp. 75–129.

Griffith, John R. *The Well-Managed Community Hospital*, 4th Edition. Chicago: Health Administration Press, 1999, pp. 117–148.

Griffith, John R. *The Moral Challenges of Healthcare Management*. Chicago: Health Administration Press, 1993.

Kovner, Anthony R., and Alan H. Channing. *A Career Guide for the Health Services Manager*, 3rd Edition. Chicago: Health Administration Press, 1999.

Zuckerman, Howard S., and William C. Dowling. "The Managerial Role." *Essentials of Health Care Management*, Albany, NY: Delmar, 1997, pp. 30–54.

Case 1

A New Faculty Practice Administrator for the Department of Medicine

Anthony R. Kovner

Sandra Compson was leaving her position as faculty practice administrator at Wise Medical Center to raise a family. Dr. Sam Bones, chief of medicine, asked Compson before leaving to become involved in the selection of her replacement.

Wise Medical Center is regarded as one of the largest and best-managed hospitals in Eastern City. The CEO, Dr. Worthy, was appointed in 1988. He has captained the dramatic growth of the medical center, its financial success, and the improvement of its medical teaching programs. Over the last five years, almost all the clinical chiefs have been replaced. Internal medicine is the largest department in the medical center. Dr. Bones is a specialist in cardiovascular disease and has an excellent reputation as a clinician.

His department has grown very large, and Bones has difficulty in staffing the large number of beds with medical residents. Bones is praised for his leadership skills, his intelligence, and his caring for those who work with him. He has been criticized for his unwillingness to make tough decisions regarding the economics of the department and for not getting rid of physicians who don't or won't meet his own and the department's high standards of quality. The medical center and the department face stiff financial pressures, and Dr. Worthy and others are trying to determine what the medical center's response to managed care should be. The medical center currently has only referral arrangements with several large health maintenance organizations (HMO).

The faculty practice in the department of medicine was formally launched three years ago in 1997, as were faculty practices in other medical departments.

Approximately 45 physicians and 13 medical sub-specialties use the faculty practice suite. The faculty practice staff includes the following: two receptionists, one secretary, three medical technicians, and one administrator. Larger physician practices including infectious disease, urology, and radiation oncology bring secretarial support when the physicians are seeing patients in the suite.

Ambulatory care facilities of the group include ten examining rooms, appropriate supporting areas for reception and waiting, a small laboratory, a technician's area, a billing office, and an office for the administrator. The space is often overcrowded, yet sometimes underutilized. Most physicians have block-time appointments and Compson has estimated that they use only 50 percent of the block time to actually see patients, while other physicians complain that they cannot get faculty practice plan (FPP) suite time to see their patients.

Compson is not privy to the revenue figures for the faculty practice, as billing is done separately by the hospital's finance department.

The FPP suite is open 9 a.m. to 5 p.m. Monday through Friday. Visits have increased from 1,500 per month in 1997 to 3,000 per month in 1999. Demand is such that if more staff and space were available, another 1,500 visits per month might be carried out with little or no targeted marketing.

The computerized billing system is not kept in the suite but terminal access is available. The physicians' offices have no knowledge of group finances. Registration and scheduling are not computerized. There is no room in the suite for chart storage. The physicians' offices must schedule their own patient appointments. Physicians are seeing two patients an hour when in proper facilities they could be seeing three. Physicians do not have their own rooms but rotate according to room availability.

The original operating concept of the faculty practice suite was as a place with an upscale ambiance where physicians could see their patients. The purpose for creating the suite was to recover scattered examination space throughout the medical center and to take advantage of economies of shared space. Based on these concepts, decisions were made early to maximize treatment space at the expense of chart storage space.

An HMO recently approached Compson seeking pediatric ambulatory care and guaranteeing 200 visits per month. But no space was available to accommodate this demand, which Compson believes could have been negotiated as a profitable service.

Bones's last interview with Compson went as follows:

Bones: Sandra, as you know, you've done a splendid job here this past year and we'll be sorry to lose you. The situation of the departmental faculty practice as I see it is this: During the past few years the practice has been organized and it has grown dramatically. We seem to be having a lot of operating problems, such as space, poor support for the physicians, and antiquated billing and scheduling systems. The question now is, what kind of a job needs to be done by the group administrator and who should we look at? What do you think?

Compson: Well, Dr. Bones, as you know, I've enjoyed tremendously the opportunity to work with you and with the members of the department and I will be sorry to leave, although I am looking forward very much to raising a family. I think that the kind of person you need is not necessarily the type of person you needed three years ago. Then you needed someone who could "put out fires" and try to keep the place working. Now I think you need a systems person who can make the place run more effectively, at the same time keeping up the morale of the staff and working with the physicians.

Bones: I agree with you. I want someone personable and energetic, who isn't afraid of work, who can get along with the doctors and the hospital administration. I think the most important thing is getting our physicians the kind of support they need to run a first-class faculty practice. The systems aren't working down there. The department isn't making the kind of money that it should be making, and we should be making it much more pleasant for our physicians to practice here. (See Illustration 1.1 for Faculty Practice Suite Billings and Collections, and Illustration 1.2 for Faculty Practice Suite Quarterly Statistics.)

Compson: As you know, per your instructions, I've started the interviewing process and will send you all the good candidates. I have spoken to several directors of programs of healthcare administration and to the hospital human resources department. There aren't a lot of good

ILLUSTRATION 1.1
Faculty Practice Suite Billings and Collections, Calendar Year 1999

Month	Billings	Collections	Gross Collection Rate
January	$308,076	$147,784	47.97%
February	$245,703	$142,090	57.83%
March	$245,211	$144,944	59.11%
April	$200,008	$171,407	85.70%
May	$301,075	$164,658	54.69%
June	$220,726	$165,677	75.06%
July	$259,163	$170,374	65.74%
August	$288,244	$159,860	55.46%
September	$248,275	$178,932	72.07%
YTD total	$2,316,481	$1,445,726	62.42%

ILLUSTRATION 1.2
Faculty Practice Suite Quarterly Statistics: Departmental
Key Indicators, July 1, 1999—September 30, 1999

Item	This Period 1991	This Period 1992	YTD 1991	YTD 1992
Percent Overall Utilization	64	72	64	72
# MDs Participation	44	50	44	50
Monthly Visits	5,280	6,528	15,840	19,584
Total Income	$320,121	$488,851	$960,363	$1,445,726
Net Income/Less Expenses	$13,755	($1,658)	$34,991	$4,568

people available with systems and management experience in healthcare. I don't want someone who is strictly a systems person. The manager must be in touch with the needs, wants, requirements, and expectations of the customers. I see the customers of the faculty practice as both the physicians and the patients.

Bones: Sandra, I agree with you there. I know you'll excuse me, but I have to attend an important strategic planning meeting for the hospital. I still don't quite understand what they're going to do, but I wish they'd give more emphasis in the plan to building up the medical center's research capabilities.

Compson: All right. Then I'll be getting back to you soon. I will make appointments with Renee, your secretary, for all the promising candidates.

One month after Sandra Compson's interview with Bones, she has completed interviews with 11 candidates for the position. She has eliminated from consideration four graduates from health administration programs who lack appropriate work experience and three medical center employees in the finance department who she feels would not relate well to the physicians in the group. Compson has made tape recordings of all her interviews with the remaining four promising candidates and has had difficulty in choosing among them.

Compson's first interview was with Dave O'Brien, currently assistant director for patient accounts in finance at the medical center. The second interview was with Sal Sorrentino, a June graduate from the City University program in health policy and management and assistant director of a neighborhood health center prior to entering the graduate program. The third interview was with Marcia Rabin, a classmate of Sorrentino's at City University and director of human resources at a 200-bed nursing home prior to entering the graduate program. The final candidate was Bonnie Goldsmith, who has just completed two years with the Department of Health and Human Services (DHHS) in Washington, DC, after graduating with a master in health administration (MHA) from City. Compson has decided to review the tapes with Dr. Tim Brass, director of the medical center's continuous quality improvement program, who also practices in the faculty practice suite, before forwarding her recommendations to Bones.

DAVID O'BRIEN

Compson (to Brass): The first interview is with Dave O'Brien, age 25. He wears conservative glasses and dresses conservatively. When I spoke to Barbara Karen, Wise Medical Center senior vice president of finance, she said that Dave was energetic and conscientious, and that he got things done. She recommended Dave highly for the position. If he has any weakness, Karen said that Dave was a hard driver, which sometimes antagonized the people under him. Dave had no problems, it seems, in getting along with his boss but not a lot of experience, if any, in working with physicians. (Compson plays a tape of the interview.)

Compson: Dave, can you tell me in a few words something about your background and experience?

O'Brien: Sure, Ms. Compson. I went to Upstate College where I was a business major. Then I started working in the hospital finance department as a biller and last year was appointed as assistant director in patient accounts. I intend to get my graduate degree at City University, in their MHA program.

Compson: Going at night?

O'Brien: Well, I don't think there will be any problem. Others have done it here at the medical center, and I want to get out of finance and into management.

Compson: Dave, what would you say has been your greatest accomplishment in patient accounts?

O'Brien: Well, Ms. Compson, I would say that I've really improved the system for billing and collections, starting with getting the bills out on time, all the way through to collections, and in refining and improving the data system that indicates how well we are doing. Performance has improved since I've taken the job—in speed, in accuracy, in the percentage collected, and in the time it takes for the hospital to get our money.

Compson: Dave, that does sound impressive. If you were faculty practice administrator, what would you consider to be your greatest asset?

O'Brien: I would say it's my ability to get a job done. There are too many people in this field who are just willing to go along with the way things have always been done until there's pressure from some quarter, and then it's often too late to do something, or to do it the right way.

Compson: And what would you say is your greatest liability?

O'Brien: Well, you know, in every organization some people are against change, because either it affects their own interest or because they just don't like change. After all, every change in somebody's department has to affect everyone involved in a relative if not in an absolute way. As my old teacher used to say, "You don't make an omelet without breaking eggs." And I guess I must rub some people the wrong way who are against what I'm doing or about to do.

Compson: What aspect of the job in the faculty practice do you think is most important?

O'Brien: I think it's improving the net revenues. I've spoken with the billing clerk in the practice and she thinks the doctors could vastly improve utilization of the facility by making changes in the block scheduling, so that docs aren't allocated time slots if they're not using them effectively. Also, the reports generated by the practice could be greatly improved. I'd like to track physician productivity in dollars relative to the opportunity costs involved in their using examining room space.

Compson: Before you go, is there anything you would like to ask me about the job?

O'Brien: As a matter of fact there is. We've talked about the salary and the benefits, but if I perform as expected, what is the likelihood of a decent increase after the first year? You know I have a wife and two young children.

Compson: Well, I'd say the chances are pretty good. Dr. Bones is fair and I think would be generous if the practice results improved significantly. (She turns off the tape recorder.)

Brass: He seems like a fine candidate.

SALVATORE SORRENTINO

Compson (to Brass): Sal Sorrentino is the next candidate. Sal is 27. He is presentable, although he dresses a bit on the flashy side—fast talking and enthusiastic. When I spoke to his reference, Dr. Plotkin of the neighborhood health center, he recommended Sal highly for the position. He said that Sal was idealistic, energetic, and pleasant. If there was any weakness, Dr. Plotkin thought that Dr. Bones should make sure that Sal realizes that he must check with him before initiating any policy or taking policy action. Nothing serious. I asked him what he meant, but Dr. Plotkin couldn't remember anything specific other than Sorrentino's setting up an appointment for Plotkin to talk with a community group about opening a satellite health center without clearing it through Plotkin first. But this had been during his first few months on the job, and Dr. Plotkin repeated that he recommended Sal highly. (Compson plays a tape of the interview.)

Compson: Sal, can you tell me in a few words something about your background and experience?

Sorrentino: Yes, I can. I was a political science major at City University, then I got involved with various community groups. While working with St. Angelo's Church, I was active in trying to improve the availability of maternal and child health services to the Latino population; as a result, I met the assistant director for community relations at the neighborhood health center. We talked and really hit it off. We were both vitally concerned with helping people in difficulty, and in making a bureaucracy work in helping patients rather than merely serving the needs of the staff. Well, I guess he liked me a lot, and before long I was offered a position as administrative assistant. After working for two years at the neighborhood health center, I was fortunate in securing a scholarship so that I could attend the City graduate program in health policy and management.

Compson: And what would you say, Sal, was your greatest accomplishment at the neighborhood health center?

Sorrentino: Well, one of the things I am proudest of is the community health fair I planned and organized. We involved community groups of all ethnic and work-related backgrounds and got the health professionals to man the booths at the fair. We worked with business corporations to get prizes and literature, on proper nutrition, for example. We conducted screening examinations for eye problems and provided TB (tuberculosis) and Pap tests. We followed up on all patients who needed help after the fair was over. The fair was well-attended and many people learned for the first time about the services the center had to offer. Of course, I accomplished a lot of other things, such as implementing a new billing system at the satellite of the neighborhood health center.

Compson: Tell me more about that.

Sorrentino: It wasn't so much really. But we needed to get more information than we were getting about patients coming for service. We had to make an effort to collect from those patients who could pay something and to have records that were suitable for reporting purposes. It was hard to implement because the staff was more interested in the patients getting service than in collecting the money.

Compson: I see. In the position we have been talking about, what do you think would be your greatest asset?

Sorrentino: Well, I see the highest priority for the group as that of attracting more patients. As my father told me, the way you make money in a business is primarily by increasing revenue rather than cutting back on expenses. I think the practice could improve rapport with patients and make changes in the suite so that the setting would be more attractive and comfortable for them. I think the practice would probably need an attractive brochure. The waiting area should be spruced up. I think the patient should know in advance how much services will cost. I'd like to devote part of my time to developing relationships with HMOs and managed care plans to increase referrals. I think the practice could benefit by extending the hours of operation. I think the suite should at least be open on Saturday mornings and one evening besides.

Compson: That sounds like an excellent idea. I've been pushing for Saturday hours also, but we aren't using our full capacity during the week as it is now. Another question, Sal, what do you think would be your greatest liability, if any, if you were chosen for the position?

Sorrentino: I don't know. I want to get things done in a hurry, I guess. I'm eager for results. Maybe I have a tendency to move a little too fast. Not really. It's hard to talk of one's faults. I really think that I can, would be able to do the job perfectly well, and I'd like the opportunity to do so. I'm not always that good at following through on all the little details of an operation. But I'm excellent at working with people who will see to all the details.

Compson: I'm a little sorry to hear that because I think a lot of details are involved in this work.

Sorrentino: I didn't mean to say that I didn't like detail work or that I wasn't good at it. I would just say that it's a relative weakness—I really prefer the other kind of work I was describing rather than doing the billing clerk's work for her.

Compson: I see. What do you think is the most important aspect of the job we've been talking about in terms of the work that needs to be done?

Sorrentino: I guess first you have to get all your systems working properly, use of the suite, billing, and reporting; and I think next the most important thing is to increase revenues. I think part of Dr. Bones's plan for the department is for the faculty practice to finance research by supporting faculty salaries that wouldn't otherwise be available.

Compson: You're right there. Is there anything now you want to ask me about the job, before you go up and talk to Dr. Bones?

Sorrentino: Two things really. First, what kind of person is Dr. Bones to work for? And, second, do you think there are good opportunities in management to further advance from this position?

Compson: In answer to your first question, I think Dr. Bones is an excellent person to work for, so long as you produce for him. He's loyal, gives you enough autonomy. Perhaps my only complaint is that it is sometimes difficult to see him, or rather that I have felt that he is such a busy man that I don't want to bother him with things I would like to discuss. I have recommended to him that he appoint another physician within the department as head of the faculty practice, at which time access to Dr. Bones will be less difficult. As to your second question, yes, I think the medical center is a large employer of people like yourself and that you can make a lot of useful contacts here. Also I feel that ambulatory care is the place to be in healthcare management in the future. (She turns off the tape.)

Brass: Well, these first two candidates have quite contrasting backgrounds. Yet it seems clear to me that either of them might do a perfectly respectable job, although of course the outcomes resulting from their work might be quite different.

MARCIA RABIN

Compson (to Brass): Yes, that's so. The third candidate is Marcia Rabin. Marcia is 24, attractive and peppy. Les Carson, director of human resources at Partners Nursing Homes, recommended her highly for the position. Ms. Rabin was director of human resources at the Brant unit. Carson said she was hard-working, gets along well with professional and nonprofessional staff. If there is any fault to find with her, Carson said it was that Rabin takes her work too seriously, drives herself too hard, and then may be absent for a few days, largely because she has difficulty in determining priorities. But Carson stressed that Rabin has performed very well on all the big jobs that he has given her to do, that she was reliable and competent. (Compson plays a tape of the interview.)

Compson: Ms. Rabin, can you tell me in a few words something about your background and experience?

Rabin: Certainly, I guess, you don't want me to go back to high school, but I was president of my student government at Suburban High. In college I majored in psychology, and for a while I thought I would like to be a psychologist. But my father works in a hospital; he is director of housekeeping at Sisters Hospital, and he encouraged me to go into healthcare management. After attending the City graduate program, I worked for two years as director of human resources at the Brant unit. Previously they didn't have a department of human resources, but when the nursing home merged with Partners, a department was established. I had worked a year previously in the department at Partners under Mr. Carson's supervision.

Compson: What would you say was your greatest accomplishment as director of human resources?

Rabin: Really, I think it was my ability to fill all the entry-level jobs, or rather to keep filling them. Also, we started and finished a job classification system under my supervision, and inaugurated an annual pay increment schedule that I think worked more fairly than the previous system. I think my real accomplishment was in legitimating the department of human resources in the nursing home where such a department had never existed before. This meant being able to service other departments and to accomplish jobs for them that used to take up a lot of their time or that they couldn't do as well before.

Compson: That sounds interesting. In terms of the present position with Dr. Bones, what would you say was your greatest asset?

Rabin: I don't know exactly how to answer that question. My first response would be to say I like and am good at doing systems work—creating order out of chaos and working effectively with people so that they feel it is their system, not something that I pushed on them. Of course, this is difficult to do because, in my case, the departments had to accept the human resources system we established; it's the only way to do things as part of a large organization. But at least the pacing and some of the details were left to them, and first we proved that we really could be of help to them.

Compson: And what, if you'll pardon my asking, would you say is your greatest liability?

Rabin: Well, if you must know, Ms. Compson, I'm not aggressive enough. Sometimes I think my efforts aren't properly appreciated, and I don't push myself to the front the way some people do. I work hard and I work well and it annoys me, sometimes more than it should, that others who don't work so hard and do so well push themselves forward and move ahead faster.

Compson: What aspect of the job, as I have tried to outline it to you, would you say is the most important, I mean at this time in the history of the faculty practice?

Rabin: I think you have to set up more clearly defined ways of doing things, *systems* if you prefer the word. I noted in the materials that you shared with me that your collection rate isn't what it should be and that your utilization of examining rooms is well below capacity also. I don't think that this kind of systems work is so different from my work in human resources, plus I have taken a few courses in quantitative analysis and feel pretty comfortable with numbers.

Compson: Are there any questions that you would like to ask me?

Rabin: Well, one question is how have the physicians, most of them men, related to having a woman in this position; second, when can you let me know if you are offering me the job? I have been offered a job as assistant director of human resources at King Hospitals, and although they aren't pressing me that hard, I would like to be able to tell them something soon.

Compson: With regard to the first question, sure, some of the physicians don't give you the respect as a manager that you would like to have, but I don't know to what extent this has to do with my being a woman. I think being a woman also has its advantages, with some of the docs. To answer your second question, I think it will take about a month for Dr. Bones to decide on a candidate. I can't tell you what you should say to the King people. You are one of the four candidates whom I am sending on to see Dr. Bones. (She turns off the tape.)

BONNIE GOLDSMITH

Compson (to Brass): I don't know, Tim. Permit me to introduce our last candidate, Bonnie Goldsmith. She dresses conservatively and gives the impression of a modest, unassuming, kindly, young woman of 27. Her boss, Dr. Muldoon, who recently left the DHHS, recommended Bonnie very highly for the position we have in mind. He described Bonnie as hard working, modest, and reliable. He said that Bonnie gets along well with people. If she has any weakness, Bonnie lacks drive and has a tendency to check with her boss about every little thing. However, Dr. Muldoon says that once a task is clearly outlined, Bonnie takes the bit between her teeth and doesn't let up. He praised highly Bonnie's staff work on the recent Task Force on the Aging Report. (She plays a tape of the interview.)

Compson: Bonnie, can you tell me a few words about your background and experience?

Goldsmith: Yes, I was a zoology major at City University. Originally, I wanted to be a physician. In fact, I attended medical school for one year, then decided it just wasn't for me. My father's a psychiatrist. I didn't know what I wanted to do. I don't know why but I thought that working in a hospital admitting department might be interesting, and I did that for a while. The administrator is a good friend of my father's, and he talked to me and convinced me to apply to City University's graduate program in health policy and management. Back in school I really enjoyed courses in continuous quality improvement, information systems, and statistics. A whole new world opened up to me, although I must confess I had a bit of difficulty with some of the heavy reading and writing courses. After graduation, I was fortunate to get a position with the Department of Health and Human Services. My father's connections helped there. I've been working for two years at DHHS doing mostly staff work, learning a lot, and I've done quite a bit of traveling.

Compson: What would you say has been your greatest accomplishment at DHHS?

Goldsmith: I would say it was the staff work I did on the President's Task Force on the Aging. I went into a lot of nursing homes and other chronic care institutions and saw what a lousy deal most of our aged get. It isn't so much this way in Europe, which I visited a couple of years ago with my father. In Europe, the homes are more like residences and fewer people go into homes. When they do go, they can take their furniture with them, and it doesn't cost as much.

Compson: What kind of solutions did you come up with?

Goldsmith: Well, it's a pretty difficult problem. I mean the part about making it possible not to have to institutionalize the elderly. I guess there are tax incentives which could be passed to allow people to keep their relatives at home. Also, more people should be able to bring their relatives into homes for day care activities and to institutionalize them for a week or two each year if necessary, either because the aged member of the household is sick or because other members of the household want a rest. Of course, we need better regulation of nursing homes to set standards for care and to establish closer relations between homes and hospitals.

Compson: I see. What do you think would be your greatest asset in the position that exists here within the department of medicine?

Goldsmith: I don't know. Perhaps it's my ability to get along with and to understand the needs and problems of the medical profession. I don't have a big ego. I like analytical work, solving operations problems, and I think I'm pretty persistent in trying to solve them.

Compson: And your greatest liability?

Goldsmith: Well, some people think I'm not aggressive enough. I don't know what this means, really, unless it is forcing your opinions on others. I guess I'm not a great innovator, and I don't like to work that much. I mean I work hard, but I don't want work to be an obsession, like it is for my father. I mean that I'm married, with a nice husband and a young son, and I want to enjoy my work and do well, but I also want to enjoy my family. I guess you could call it a lack of ambition. But I think this country needs more people like me, people whose satisfaction comes from a job well done rather than striving for money, status, and power. I'm intellectually committed to group practice as a better way to deliver healthcare, and I'd like to do my part to see that primary care is improved in this country. So this may be a liability or an asset, I don't know.

Compson: I'm not sure either. But certainly if you do the job well, what you say makes sense. Well, enough of that; what aspects of the job strike you as most important?

Goldsmith: Well, I don't know. Certainly, the practice has to be organized systematically, and billing has to be improved. I'd like to track these processes scientifically, see what the standards are and should be, track the variance from standards by analyzing all the steps in these processes, and then work with all the individuals involved from physicians to receptionists in improving these systems. This might require a number of meetings, and I don't know how feasible such meetings would be because of people's time requirements. There are a few questions I would like to ask you.

Compson: Please go ahead.

Goldsmith: My first question is, do you think the faculty practice is going to grow? The second is incidental, but I would like to know more about the benefits, such as tuition remission, as I was thinking of furthering my education at City, perhaps taking some more courses in statistical analysis.

Compson: I think the faculty practice will continue to grow. Space is our key constraint now, and the medical center will have to figure out how we are going to better deal with managed care. Also, should we eventually combine the faculty practice plans in the various departments into one multidisciplinary group practice that is also in the managed care business? Of course this all has to be squared with the department's ambitious goals in teaching and research. Sometimes, despite the excellent reputation of the medical center and the quality of its leadership, I wonder if we can possibly excel in all these different areas as well as in all of the leading areas of clinical medicine. With respect to your second question, yes, I believe tuition remission for such purposes is available, although I don't see where you will have the time to fit everything in with the demands of this job, which are quite considerable, and with your family obligations. (She turns off the tape.)

Brass: Well, Sandy, now all you have to do is tell Dr. Bones whom you recommend for the job.

Compson: I need to sleep on it. This assignment has given me more problems than I bargained for, but that's the joy of working, isn't it, Tim, solving these problems?

Brass: I agree with you there. Sorry, but I've got to leave now. I want to think about this some more and I'll give you my opinion tomorrow.

Case 2

The Associate Director and the Controllers

Anthony R. Kovner

Fortunately for Jim Joel, he didn't lose his temper often. Otherwise, he might not have been able to function as associate director of the Morris Health Care Program of the Nathan D. Wise Medical Center (see Illustration 2.1). But now, he had become so enraged at the Morris program controller, Percy Oram, that he had to concentrate hard to keep from yelling. Joel had just been informed by Felix Schwartzberg, an assistant director, that the accounting department was not collecting cash from the billing assistants in the family health units as previously agreed. Unfortunately, Oram did not usually keep Joel informed of his actions. But in any case, Joel knew his own reaction was excessive—an aspiring health services executive did not throw a tantrum, which is what he now felt like doing.

Joel is 30 years old, ambitious, a recent graduate from Ivy University's master in health care administration program. Before returning to school, he had worked as a registered representative on Wall Street, where he had found the work remunerative but uninteresting. The director of the Ivy program, Dr. Leon Russell, assumed the post of director of the Nathan D. Wise Medical Center in 1966. Joel, one of his best students, asked to join Russell toward the end of that year, and he was hired shortly thereafter as an assistant hospital administrator. The Nathan D. Wise Medical Center is located in New York City and comprises three large programs: the Nathan D. Wise Hospital, the Lennox Rehabilitation Center, and the Morris Health Care Program. The hospital and the rehabilitation center are owned by the Wise Medical Center, but the Morris Health Care

ILLUSTRATION 2.1
Organization Chart: Nathan D. Wise Medical Center

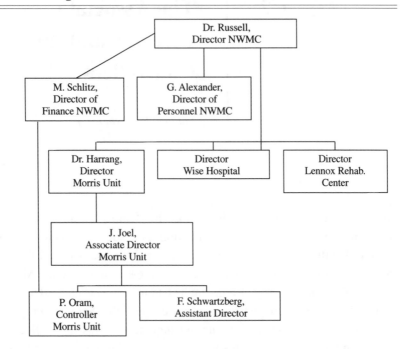

Program is operated by the Wise Medical Center under contract with the City of New York and is located in a city-owned facility.

Russell had been impressed with his former student's drive and promise and had originally created a job for Joel. This included half-time as a staff assistant at Wise Hospital and half-time as an evaluator at the Morris Unit, where new methods of delivering ambulatory medical care were being developed and demonstrated. However, the director of the Morris Unit, Dr. Lawrence White, had resigned to become commissioner of health of a Midwestern city, and six months later, his associate director, Mr. Phillip Bright, had announced his intention to resign to join White. By March 1967, Russell had already hired a replacement for White, Dr. Miller Harrang, a 45-year old physician, who had previously been medical director of the Ochs Ambulatory Care Unit in another part of New York State. Since Joel was not being fully utilized at Wise Hospital, although he had performed capably whatever he had been asked to do,

Russell decided to offer him the position of associate director of the Morris Unit.

Joel felt ambivalent regarding Russell's offer. He knew he would take the position, even before requesting a night to think it over, but at the same time he had certain reservations. Joel was enjoying his work at the hospital. He had submitted an in-depth plan for increasing efficiency of the operating room, which had been enthusiastically accepted by the medical staff executive committee, and he was just starting an evaluation of patient transport in the hospital. His key interest was implementation of his master's thesis on nurse staffing. Joel believed that by assigning rooms to patients on the basis of their nursing needs, one-third fewer registered nurses would be required. Joel wished to be director of a large general hospital within ten years. He wasn't sure how working at the Morris Unit would advance him toward that goal, nor how comfortable he would feel working in a facility serving the poor in a slum section of the city.

However, after taking the job, Joel found before long that he liked working at the Morris Unit immensely. Morris was rapidly expanding— in the last year, the number of physician visits had increased 25 percent to 215,000. Through a generous grant from the Office of Economic Opportunity (OEO), the budget had increased from $1.5 million to $2.5 million. Joel worked 65 to 70 hours a week. There was so much to do. He liked Harrang, his present boss, and he liked the people who worked at Morris. The atmosphere was busy and informal, a nice change of pace from the Wise Hospital where things happened more slowly. Dramatic change was the norm at Morris, whether this was conversion of the medical and pediatric clinics to family health units, or confrontations with a community health council resulting in increased participation in policymaking by the poor. There was no formal division of responsibility between Harrang and Joel. Harrang spent most of his time in community relations (time-consuming and frustrating), in individual conversations with members of the medical staff at Morris, and in working out problems with the Wise Hospital. Harrang also took responsibility for certain medical units such as the emergency room, obstetrics-gynecology (ob-gyn), and psychiatry. Joel's primary responsibility lay in the area of staff activities such as finance, personnel, and purchasing. He also supervised several departments or units, including laboratory, x-ray, pharmacy, dental, housekeeping, and maintenance. Responsibility for the family health units was shared by the two top administrators.

Under the former top administrators, White and Bright, the Morris Unit had been run as a unit independent from the Wise Hospital. The unit was decentralized, with departments such as laboratory and internal medicine handling their own personnel and often their own purchasing. It was Russell's wish to create a more integrated medical center, and Joel saw an important part of his job as creating staff departments (such as personnel and purchasing) and upgrading these functions with the help of medical center experts.

When Joel arrived, the controller's department consisted of four individuals: Bill Connor, the controller, who promptly resigned (Joel never met this individual whom he was told had personal problems of an unspecified nature); Peter Stavrogin, an industrious bookkeeper, who was a 55-year-old East European refugee with a limited knowledge of English; a payroll clerk; and a secretary. This was the staff for an organization of more than 400 employees that was funded by five different agencies under five different contracts. The accounting department had heavy personnel responsibilities as well, at least so far as payroll was concerned, because no personnel department as such existed. One of the first things Joel did was to hire Connor's replacement. In doing so—and to conform with Russell's policy of an integrated medical center—Joel enlisted the help of the medical center staff: Milton Schlitz, the director of financial affairs, and Grover Alexander, the director of personnel. Alexander volunteered to place the ads and check the references of applicants for the controller position, and Schlitz suggested that he screen the applicants. The best three or four would then be reviewed by Joel and Harrang who, between them, would select the new controller. Joel was pleased with this arrangement, although he thought the recommended salary for the position was too low. He agreed to go along, however, based on the recommendations of Alexander and Schlitz, who had considerably more experience in these matters.

However, because of what Schlitz and Alexander believed to be a shortage of qualified accountants, and the undesirable location of Morris, they found only two prospective applicants. Albert Fodor, a 55-year-old certified public accountant (CPA), with no hospital experience but good references, was the obvious first choice to be Morris's new controller.

Fodor was pleasant and industrious. It took him six months to learn the job. Fodor then resigned, citing that the tremendous pressure and workload were too great for a man of his years. The payroll clerk also resigned at this time for a higher-paying job at another hospital.

During the next three months, Joel employed three new billing clerks as well as a personnel assistant and a purchasing agent. Most of the accounting department's work, which would have been done by the controller, was performed by Joel, who handled the budgetary aspects, while Stavrogin covered the accounting aspects. This system was unsatisfactory, however, because both felt Joel should spend less time troubleshooting financial problems and more time on the programmatic aspects of the job. Also, Joel wanted to conduct and supervise a variety of special studies for contract purposes and cost comparisons, an undertaking hardly feasible under the present setup.

So Joel went back to Schlitz and Alexander, insisting that the salary for the controller job be raised $3,000 per year because of the complexity of the job and the distance from Schlitz's direct supervision. Schlitz agreed reluctantly; he knew he would have to raise salaries or face morale problems in the accounting department at Wise Hospital.

After an intensive advertising program, eight to ten candidates had been screened by Schlitz, and three candidates were sent to Joel and Harrang, of whom Perry Oram seemed the best. Oram was 40 years old, without a CPA but with solid accounting experience in a medium-sized business firm. Oram had no hospital or healthcare experience. Schlitz and Joel did not feel that such experience was necessary for the job, although, of course, they would have preferred it. Oram was physically attractive, well-dressed, and married with no children. He said he was interested in advancing himself in the expanding hospital field. Joel went over the Fodor experience with Oram, stressing the work pressures. Oram responded that he was looking for a job where he would have more autonomy, where he was in charge and responsible, and where he knew he would be rewarded (or blamed) based on his performance. Of course, he would like to spend a lot of time at first learning the ropes with Schlitz. Joel told Oram he would let him know later that week if the job was his. Afterward, Joel and Harrang agreed that Oram was the best of the three candidates. However, Harrang had a vague feeling of unease. Oram seemed too good, too qualified for the job. Independently, Schlitz also agreed that Oram was the best of the three candidates. Alexander checked Oram's reference which confirmed the high opinion of Schlitz and Joel. Oram was then offered the job as controller of the Morris Unit, and he accepted.

From Joel's point of view, things went fairly well at first, perhaps because Joel was busy with other matters and because Oram was spending a lot of time at Wise Hospital with Schlitz. The first sign of trouble was the lateness of the monthly statement that Joel had instituted and required. The statement included detailed categories of departmental costs, comparing costs (Joel hoped eventually to compare costs with performance as well) for this month, last month, and this month last year, as well as cumulative totals for this year. Joel had reviewed with Oram how he wanted the statement done (in what categories), with a cover sheet that would suggest the reasons for any large variances. Oram agreed to furnish such a report, but one month after the month in question, Joel still hadn't received it. When asked, Oram said that he was too busy, and that he was working on it. When the statement finally did arrive on Joel's desk, there was no cover letter about variances, and there were large variances caused by sloppy accounting (items in one category last year, for instance, that were in another this year, causing large discrepancies). Even some of the amounts were incorrect, where salaries of certain individuals had not been counted in the proper categories. Joel, patiently but with irritation, explained that this was not what he wanted. He told Oram why he wanted what he wanted, and when he wanted the report—15 days after the end of the month. Timeliness, he emphasized, was especially important because, although the city contract remained at the same sum every year, changes in the OEO budget had to be individually approved by Washington, and OEO funds had to be spent by the year's end. This meant that a lot of shuffling had to be done (e.g., transfer of city positions because of increased salary costs to the OEO budget) based on correct information. Oram apologized and agreed to improve performance.

At the same time, Joel had begun to hear complaints about Oram from other staff members. Linda Lee, the personnel assistant, and Felix Schwartzberg, the assistant director, complained about his rudeness, arrogance, and insensitivity to the poor—like his repeated statements about "welfare chiselers." Such terminology was at odds with the philosophy of the unit. When changes in employee paychecks had to be made because of supervisory mistakes or because of inadequate notice concerning an employee's vacation, Oram reluctantly did the extra work. He warned those involved, without clearing it with Joel, that eventually checks would not be issued on this basis.

Joel had been approached by Oram two weeks previously about a personal matter. Oram explained that he had to come to work an hour and a half late twice a week because of an appointment with his psychiatrist. The psychiatrist couldn't see him before or after work, and he hoped Joel would be sympathetic. Oram was willing to stay late to make up the time. Joel said he wanted to think it over before responding, and then discussed Oram's situation with Schlitz and Harrang. They all agreed that they would have liked to have known this before Oram was hired, but that if the work was done and he made up the time, it would be permitted. It was agreed that Joel would check occasionally in the accounting office, which was located in a separate building a block away from the health services facility, to see if Oram was indeed putting in the extra time.

For about the next six months, Oram's performance remained essentially the same. The cover letter was superficial, and the statements were late and often contained mistakes. (The statements did, however, eventually arrive and were eventually corrected.) The special studies requested of Oram were done late and Joel often had to redo them. In checking on Oram, Joel never found him in the office after 5:00 p.m., but he did not check every day. The routine work of the accounting department was being done effectively, but this had been the case before the current situation with Oram, when no controller had been present. Oram had added another clerk, and Joel suspected that Stavrogin was still performing much of the supervisory work as he had been previous to Oram's arrival. Joel was not happy. He discussed the situation with Harrang, who agreed that the statements were less than acceptable. Harrang told Joel to do as he liked, but to clear it first with Schlitz.

Soon after, Joel went to Wise Hospital to discuss Oram with Schlitz. Schlitz, a CPA, had been controller of Wise Hospital, now Wise Medical Center, for 27 years. Schlitz was talkative but often vague, hard-working, basically conservative, and oriented primarily to the needs of Wise Hospital (at least in Joel's opinion) rather than to the Medical Center at large. This was reflected in the allocation of overhead in the Morris contracts (e.g., administrative time allocated was greater than that actually provided) and in the high price of direct services, such as laboratory, performed for Morris by the hospital. More important, Schlitz saw his job almost exclusively as worrying about "the bottom line"—whether the hospital or the Morris Unit ran a deficit or broke even—rather than in terms of performance relative to costs. Nevertheless, Joel thought he had established a cordial relationship with Schlitz, and their discussion about Oram was indeed cordial for the most part. Schlitz agreed that Oram's performance left something to be desired. He was particularly unhappy about the time Oram put in. On the other hand, Schlitz felt that the Morris Unit was in good financial shape and that there was nothing to worry about. In view of the experience with the previous controller, Fodor, Schlitz wondered if indeed they could find a better man for the salary. Schlitz urged that they talk to Oram together but said that he would go along with whatever Joel wanted to do.

Acting on Schlitz's recommendation, Joel set up a meeting with Schlitz, Oram, and Harrang to discuss his dissatisfactions. During the course of the meeting Joel did admit that the monthly statements were improving, but only after extensive prodding. Oram remarked that the reason for this meeting surprised him; he had thought, on the basis of previous meetings with Joel and Schlitz, that they were pleased with his work. He then asked, in fact, to be included in more top-level policy meetings, as he felt that controllers should be part of the top management group. Oram said he felt isolated, which resulted in part from the location of the accounting department in a separate building. Joel responded that he would welcome Oram's participation in policy meetings after the work of the accounting department had been sufficiently upgraded, and that Oram would be kept informed of and invited to all meetings that concerned his department.

Returning to the Morris facility, Joel discussed his perplexity with Harrang. Actually, he asserted, he did not understand what was going on here. Oram never gave him what he wanted. He had no way of knowing how busy Oram actually was. Lately, Oram had said that he couldn't produce certain studies by the stipulated dates because he was busy doing work for Schlitz or attending meetings at the hospital with Schlitz and the controllers of the other units of the medical center.

Harrang replied that he believed that Schlitz was indeed responsible in part for Oram's lack of responsiveness. Schlitz had probably told Oram not to listen to Joel but to do what he, Schlitz, recommended, because Oram's salary and benefits were largely determined by Schlitz rather than by Joel. Schlitz didn't want the accounting department at Morris to use more sophisticated techniques than the hospital because this would reflect badly on Schlitz. Moreover, Schlitz wanted his "own man" at the Morris Unit so that the hospital benefited in all transactions with Morris (e.g., there should be enough slack in the city budget to meet any contingency, with as many staff as possible switched to the OEO budget).

Joel had to agree with Harrang's observation. But on the other hand, Harrang had become increasingly bitter toward Russell over the last six months. This concerned a variety of matters, most specifically Harrang's salary. Harrang was working much harder than he had bargained for at Morris, and he didn't feel he was getting the money or the credit he deserved. Nevertheless, Joel did think that Schlitz might be part of the problem; he had never been particularly impressed with Schlitz.

Several weeks later, a new state regulation was passed stating that for city agencies to collect under Medicaid, all efforts must be made to collect from those who, by state edict, could afford to pay. This was in conflict with Morris's philosophy of providing free service to all who said they couldn't pay, and there was much opposition to implementation of the policy by the professionals at Morris. The professional staff felt that no special effort should be made to collect from those who had formerly received free services. Oram disagreed with this philosophy and said that Morris should make every effort to collect.

When it came to implementing collections, Oram requested that the registration staff who were to collect the money should be part of his department, or that a separate cashier's office should be set up on the first floor of the health facility. Otherwise his department didn't wish to be involved. Schwartzberg, the assistant director in charge of registration, argued that the registration staff should continue as part of the family health units because of other duties, that no space was available on the first floor for a cashier's office, and that it was not fair to patients to make them stand in two lines, as they would have to under Oram's arrangement, before seeing a health professional. Joel and Harrang sided with Schwartzberg and discussed with Oram a plan under which he would be responsible for the cash collection aspects of the registrar's work. It was agreed that Oram would devise, within a week, a plan for implementation. After two weeks, Schwartzberg reported to Joel that Oram had not devised a plan and was unwilling to cooperate with the plan Schwartzberg and the chief registrar had devised.

Joel pounded his desk. What concerned him was not so much this specific matter, which he knew he would resolve, but what to do in general with Oram. Joel was working Saturday mornings with a militant community group over next year's OEO budget and was still working 60 to 65 hours per week. He knew that it was his job to decide. He didn't think Oram's performance would improve unless Schlitz agreed with Joel's priorities and, even in that event, sufficient improvement was unlikely. On the other hand, Joel did not look forward to hiring a fourth controller in the two years he had worked at Morris. Moreover, the routine work of the accounting department was being performed to the satisfaction of Schlitz. Joel decided to go for a walk by the river and make his decision.

Short Case A | Nowhere Job

David Melman

John Ernest works for a young and growing healthcare company. The company has been successfully developing a market niche by contracting with colleges and universities to manage and operate their campus health centers. Ernest has been hired to develop the operational structure of a new product that will connect the managed care health insurance coverage of the students with their campus health center. This new product will result in cost savings and superior service delivery. It is a new concept in the industry and, while Ernest does not have significant healthcare experience, he does have a great deal of energy and enthusiasm and is expected to learn on the job.

Ernest is not given a formal job description. He is verbally given a list of performance objectives, but these objectives are changed without his input and without detailed new objectives put in their place. Ernest's work environment is unusual in that he mostly works out of a home office, with occasional trips to the corporate office 70 miles away. Ernest is told that he will report to the corporate medical director, who is located in Miami, 1,200 miles away. Communication is made by telephone, fax, and e-mail.

Ernest makes progress in achieving organizational objectives but is facing obstacles in terms of his isolation from others in the company. He is not informed of changes in project objectives, nor of the underlying reasons for these changes. Ernest finds that this isolation limits his ability to grow and contribute because he is unable to describe his company's needs accurately to outside vendors without being so informed himself.

Ernest asks to have a formal job description and stated performance objectives based on the format suggested by a human resources consultant hired by the company. He receives no response. He is asked to complete the contracts with several outside vendors he has negotiated.

Ernest is told he now reports to an outside consultant who has been hired to help coordinate technical operations, including information systems. This outside consultant tells Ernest not to proceed with these contracts the very day after the CEO has told him to complete them.

Ernest attempts to contribute to the sales and marketing efforts of his company by proposing that the company sponsor an institute at a prestigious university, and he wants to contribute his time and energy to make this project a success. He is told it is a good idea, but the vice president of sales and marketing does not keep his commitment to respond to Ernest's proposal. Ernest sends reminders and continues to develop the idea with the university. He is trying to expand his job responsibilities to include business development but needs the support of others in his organization to make a meaningful contribution.

Case Questions

1. What should Ernest do?
2. What are the risks to Ernest?
3. How could Ernest have anticipated these problems before accepting his current position?
4. What should be Ernest's priorities in evaluating an alternative career opportunity? Why?

Short Case B | Manager Morale at Uptown Hospital

Anthony R. Kovner

Date: April 1995

To: Martin Dexter, CEO

From: Paula Long, Director of Human Resources

In talking about our management development program with several participants, I received the following feedback, which I think is serious and urgent enough to bring to your attention:

1. Morale is very low because of delayed program development, no allowance for overtime or per diems, and the resultant squeeze on management.
2. The hospital suffers from lack of supervisory staff, inadequate systems support, lack of trust among employees and managers, and a lack of a forum for communication upward.
3. The hospital provides a lot of substandard care, doesn't look nice, and is not "user-friendly." There are too many employees who don't "carry their load" and who are nasty.
4. The "word" for many potential users in the minority community we serve is not use Uptown but rather to go to St. Stephen or Washington Hospitals.
5. Top management has not communicated to middle managers the strategic plan. There are no open lines of communication nor is there any shared management philosophy.
6. Good things and accomplishments by small groups aren't recognized or appreciated.
7. There is no feeling that morale will improve if financial performance improves.
8. Managers and department heads are afraid to fire someone they can't replace.

9. People are worried about their jobs.
10. No one trusts the message of the relationship with our teaching affiliate.

I have several ideas about what we should do about this, but I wanted to send this off to you right away while I continue to consider the situation.

Case Questions

1. What should CEO Dexter do in receiving Paula Long's memo?
2. How could such conditions have occurred at Uptown Hospital?
3. What constraints and opportunities does CEO Dexter face in implementing these recommendations?
4. How can CEO Dexter overcome constraints and take advantage of the opportunities?

Part II

Control

Introduction

What large managed care systems have in common, whether they be Intermountain Health Care, Columbia HCA, Kaiser Permanente, or Henry Ford Health System (to name only a few), is a clearly perceived need, backed by a commitment to spend substantial funds, to improve their computer-based management and clinical information systems, that is, their control system. This information is to be used not to centralize power at corporate headquarters, but rather to help professionals and practitioners in the system improve the quality of services provided and to lower costs.

To develop a comprehensive control system, the following elements are necessary: performance expectations to set performance guidelines; an information system to measure performance; control auspices to evaluate performance compared to expectations; an incentive system to influence producer performance; and coordinated phasing to minimize dysfunctions of the controlling auspice.[1]

If, as Peter Drucker says, "the basic problem of service institutions is not high cost but lack of effectiveness,"[2] performance expectations in health services organizations must be defined in terms of goal attainment instead of increased budget allocations. The traditional approach to control when output measures are available, as in automobile production, is to relate capital and operational costs to unit standards of production. In healthcare, costs are usually related to process activities; therefore, a control system sensitive to cost must include some assurance of quality because cost control does not inherently consider output quality. Consider, therefore, what the performance expectations are in the three cases in this section: "Healthier Babies in Twin Falls, Idaho," "Reengineering a Physician Practice," and "Organization Design for the Breast Service at Easter Medical Center."

An information system includes the techniques for gathering, recording, summarizing, and disseminating data. It also includes evaluating the information system itself: the relevance and processing of data collected, the reports generated relative to the performance expectations of the controlling auspice, and the quality and cost of the system itself. What kinds of information are the managers of the three organizations in these cases using to make decisions? What kinds of information do they require for effective decision making?

In addition, who establishes performance expectations in these three organizations? Who takes responsibility for assuming that the information system is effective and efficient? Who monitors performance and takes corrective action when appropriate? And who establishes the systems procedures necessary to contrast actual performance with relevant performance expectations?

An explicitly communicated incentive framework is fundamental to an effective control system. In healthcare, the absence of output standards means that incentives must be structured on surrogate measures of output, such as the type and quantity of patients and the type and volume of procedures performed. Effective reorienting of provider performance can result if incentives are structured on the same factors for which performance expectations exist and for which data are collected. In the three cases, consider what incentives underlie the current and future decisions of the key participants.

Coordination of phasing is the process of keeping performance in line with provider and customer expectations—not insisting on more than the producers are capable of and not promising to accomplish more than the principals in the organization can actually do. Consider to what extent the managers in these cases are realistic in their expectations and their promises, or how they should have behaved.

The three cases here present very different problems of control. Twin Falls is recognized as a leader in applying the concepts of continuous quality improvement (CQI) both within their hospital and in the community they serve. Three pillars of CQI are customer mindedness, statistical mindedness, and organizational transformation. These pillars relate to the three questions that underlie their goal to make Twin Falls the healthiest community in the country. Why do we do what we do? (Does this meet customer needs?) How do we know it works? (How do we understand and measure the process and the outcomes of care?) How can we do it better? (How do we go about creating a learning organization?)

For another view of Twin Falls, see the article by McEachern et al.[3]

Mergers in industry and healthcare appear to be easy: the boards agree; the lawyers are called in and the deal is done. That's the easy part. Fulfilling the promise of economies of scale, shared cultures, synergy, and close working relationships is more difficult by far. The case of "Reengineering a Physician Practice" raises such issues.

"Organization Design for the Breast Service at Easter Medical Center" is a case example of how to make or not to make changes in an organization. How should leaders carefully approach desired change?

Case Questions

Healthier Babies in Twin Falls, Idaho

1. What is the process that leads to healthy babies as viewed by the Twin Falls team?
2. Who is served by this process?
3. How would one measure improvement in the process and outcome?
4. What needs to be done to change the organization of care to keep improving this process?
5. What should the team do next?

Reengineering a Physician Practice

1. What should Scott recommend to the board that the physicians and staffs of the two practices do to enhance the merger?
2. What constraints and opportunities does the merged practice face as a result of their demographic and philosophical differences?
3. In what other areas can Mr. Desmond apply the systems analysis and design process?
4. What are the key factors that physicians and staff should be aware of when reengineering a newly merged practice?
5. What is the role of a manager in empowering her employees?

Organization Design for the Breast Service at Easter Medical Center

1. What are the problems of the breast service?
2. What are the causes of the problems?
3. What should Dr. Wiley do now on receiving the consultant report from Mr. Crash?

4. What are the opportunities and constrains facing Dr. Wiley if he attempts to implement the consultant's recommendations?

5. How could Dr. Wiley take advantage of the opportunities and overcome the constraints in implementation?

Notes

1.   Anthony R. Kovner and Edward J. Lusk, "State Regulation of Health Care Costs," *Medical Care* 13, no. 8 (August 1975): 619–29.

2.   Peter Drucker, "Managing the Public Service Institution," *The Public Interest* 33 (Fall 1973): 43–60.

3.   Edward J. McEachern, Duncan Neuhauser, Paul Miles, and John Bingham, "Managing Rural Health Care Reform," Chapter 8 in *Health Systems Management: Readings and Commentary*, 7th Edition, edited by Anthony R. Kovner and Duncan Neuhauser (Chicago: Health Administration Press, 2000).

Selected Bibliography

Berwick, Donald M., A. Blanton Godfrey, and Jane Roessner. *Curing Health Care: New Strategies for Quality Improvement*. San Francisco: Jossey-Bass, 1990.

Carey, Raymond G., and Robert C. Lloyd. *Measuring Quality Improvement in Health Care*. New York, NY: Quality Resources, a Division of the Kraus Organizations Limited, 1995.

Flood, A. B., J. S. Zinn, S. M. Shortell, and W. R. Scott. "Organizational Performance: Managing for Efficiency and Effectiveness," in S. Shortell and A. Kaluzny, *Health Care Management: Organization Design and Behavior*, 4th Edition, Albany NY: Delmar Publishers, 2000, pp. 356–393.

Griffith, John R. *The Well-Managed Health Care Organization*, 4th Edition. Chicago: Health Administration Press, 1999, Chapter 7.

Kovner, Anthony R., Guest Editor. (Special Issue): "Community Benefit Programs for Health Care Organizations." *The Journal of Health Administration Education* 12, no. 13 (summer 1994).

Lewis, J. E. "Improving Productivity: the Ongoing Experience of an Academic Department of Medicine," *Academic Medicine* 7, no. 4 (April 1996): 317–28.

Milio, Nancy. *Engines of Empowerment: Using Information Technology to Create Healthy Communities and Challenge Public Policy*. Chicago: Health Administration Press, 1996.

Trabin, Tom (ed.). *The Computerization of Behavioral Healthcare: How to Enhance Clinical Practice, Management, and Communications*. San Francisco: Jossey-Bass Publishers, 1996.

Case 3 | Healthier Babies in Twin Falls, Idaho

Dorothy Shaffer

Emily Blackwell is spending a summer in Twin Falls, Idaho, learning about continuous quality improvement. She has been providing staff support for Paul Miles, M.D., who chairs the hospital's project to make the area the healthiest place in America to have a baby.

Idaho, the seventh most sparsely populated state, has the lowest physician-to-population ratio in the nation (114 physicians per 100,000 people versus a national average of 184 per 100,000).[1] The state's population is one million, with 145,000 people living in Magic Valley, an agricultural-based community in south central Idaho (11,000 square miles). The Valley, composed of eight counties, has a population density of 12.2 persons per square mile (ppsm) compared to the national average of 69.4 ppsm, and two of the counties are classified as "frontier."[1] This area of Idaho is unique with its low population, lack of public transportation, and the worst low-birthweight and perinatal mortality rates in the state. In 1988, Magic Valley's low-birthweight rate was 6.6 percent with a state average of 5.1 percent. Concurrently, the perinatal mortality rate was 10.7 per 1,000 for Magic Valley and 9.2 per 1,000 for the state.[1]

Twin Falls, population 29,000, is the largest town in this eight-county region, and the city is home to the two largest hospitals in Magic Valley. The Southcentral Public Health Department is also located here. There is no managed care in the area or in the state. One of the hospitals, Twin Falls Clinic, with a 44-bed capacity, is under private ownership and is the only hospital in Idaho that is not a member of the Idaho Hospital Association. The facility provides limited services with no

The author wishes to thank Paul Miles, M.D., Duncan Neuhauser, Ph.D., and Linda Headrick, M.D., for their teaching and guidance.

general pediatrics or ob-gyn, but it does have some subspecialties unique to the area, including plastic surgery, rheumatology, and endocrinology.[2] The other hospital in Twin Falls is Magic Valley Regional Medical Center (MVRMC), a not-for-profit, county-owned hospital that serves as a secondary care institution for the eight-county region and is designated as the Medicare regional referral center. The hospital is managed by Quorum Health Resources, has a $55 million revenue, and a 165-bed capacity. There are 123 physicians with privileges at MVRMC, 80 of whom are very active. Their patient population is made up of 50 percent Medicare and 14 percent Medicaid patients.[3] Four smaller rural hospitals are also located within this region; they are staffed by family practitioners and all are under different ownership and funding. The Department of Public Health is run by the district and serves this same eight-county region. The department has a number of outlying facilities and multiple specialty and preventive health clinics within its Twin Falls office. All of the hospitals and health services have separate visions, separate patient registrations, and separate databases. Communication between these facilities is poor, and care is often duplicated.

Within this environment, healthcare resources are scarce, difficult to access, and disjointed. This is a condition not uncommon to much of America, but because Idaho has an inadequate supply of physicians and resources, the status of its healthcare cannot continue to be ignored. In 1987, the hospital board at MVRMC revised its vision statement to read, "MVRMC will be a standard of excellence and cooperation in making Magic Valley the healthiest place in America." With this change, John Bingham, the hospital administrator, introduced a new way to approach healthcare to achieve this vision. His interests were based on the Deming Management Method,[4] but he was also influenced by both Bronowski[5] and Senge.[6] The process, labeled continuous quality improvement (CQI), emphasizes cooperation, systems thinking, and an understanding of statistical variation and human interactions within a given system. This model involves a strict reliance on data collection and analysis, while using the scientific method to institute change and improvement. Deming, an American statistician whose work was closely linked to Japan's postwar economic growth, used the above ideas to transform business management and production.[4] Bingham wanted to attempt the same transformation in healthcare.

Bingham was aware that many of these ideas were broad and difficult to initiate. Nevertheless, he was driven by two fundamental questions: "Why do we do what we do? And how do we know that what we do works?" which led him to a third question: "How can we make what we do better?"[7] His shift to quality improvement and a systems view of healthcare (Illustration 3.1) was supported by the Hospital Corporation of America (HCA), the hospital's former management group before Quorum. Magic Valley Regional Medical Center became a pilot hospital of HCA for implementing quality improvement. However, even with this support, Bingham had reservations about the change in thinking because the new approach could be perceived as another fad in healthcare reform and the question still persisted of whether Deming's theories could be effective or not in the healthcare industry. Regardless, he started at the top, with the hospital board, as a way to anchor these ideas first and then incorporate them into the daily functioning of the hospitals and the surrounding community.[7] He and the hospital began accomplishing this vision by addressing parts of the system, with the continual focus on restoring and improving the community's health.

During the time of this transition, the state was involved in the Idaho Perinatal Project and had been working for eight years to address the issues of perinatal morbidity and mortality. In an effort to decrease this problem, the project's goal was to standardize the equipment and training for neonatal resuscitation across the state. They successfully improved the facilities and staff training without improving the process, and the mortality rates did not improve. As mentioned, by 1988, the state's perinatal mortality rate was 9.2 per 1,000 and the low-birthweight percentage, an indicator of neonatal morbidity, was 5.1 percent, which still left Idaho with the same problem it had attempted to fix.[1]

Dr. Paul Miles, a pediatrician in Twin Falls and member of the hospital board at MVRMC, was working with the Idaho Perinatal Project. Because of his close connection to Mr. Bingham and the MVRMC, he decided to apply the quality improvement theories to the ongoing perinatal project. Thirty-three physicians in Magic Valley provide obstetrics care, and 20 percent of the MVRMC admissions are pregnancy related. Approximately 50 percent of the total deliveries in the area were performed at MVRMC, with the majority of high-risk newborns treated in their neonatal intensive care unit (NICU).[8]

ILLUSTRATION 3.1
Systems View of Healthcare

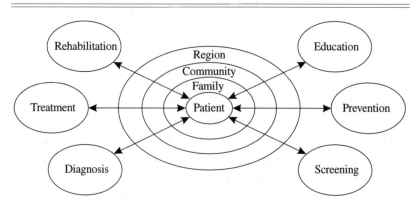

The very high risk newborns are transferred to tertiary care centers in Boise, Idaho (130 miles west) or Salt Lake City, Utah (200 miles southeast). This eight-county district, although fully up-to-date with its equipment, still had some of the worst outcome data, mentioned earlier, in one of the worst states. Within this region and using quality improvement guidelines, Miles realized the great opportunity that existed to better the health of pregnant women, newborns, and the community as a whole.

In Miles's thinking, the next step to take in solving the problem of perinatal morbidity and mortality in Idaho centered on the vision of making Magic Valley the healthiest place in America to have a baby and to cooperate with all of the care providers in the area. To achieve this goal, a systems approach was adopted, keeping in mind the strengths and weaknesses of the community while always keeping the patient at the focal point of care. Magic Valley Regional Medical Center, along with the Public Health Department and a few physicians, began looking at prevention and improvement along with treatment. They wanted to become proactive in their problem solving with an emphasis on continual learning and improving on the existing model.

Formally, the CQI plan contains a step-by-step approach in applying the scientific method to problem solving. Initially, a problem is identified and a plan for improvement is made (the hypothesis). Then, the plan is executed (testing the hypothesis). Next, the results are checked (data analysis). Finally, the results are acted upon (rethinking the hypothesis).[9]

And so, once the change has been made, its effectiveness is documented, with the aim to decrease variation within the entire system, thus making the community a healthier place in which to live. While this formal approach to problem solving provides an excellent structure to create positive changes and growth, the initial attempts at applying CQI to the perinatal project were much less formalized. Instead, a few individuals concentrated on the philosophy behind the new approach and used those theories as a guide with the hope that this type of problem solving could help the status of healthcare.

Within this structure, Miles felt that an initial step to improve peri-natal morbidity and mortality was to look upstream and concentrate on prenatal care itself, and so his hypothesis—that women who do not receive prenatal care are more likely to have high-risk infants—was tested. This statement is based on the fact that prenatal care is associated with improved perinatal morbidity, but it is unclear what aspects of prenatal care account for this association.[10] By focusing on the area of prenatal care, those involved in the project hoped to see a decrease in neonatal intensive care admissions, a decrease in long-term morbidity of children, and an increase in the overall health of the community. The team that was organized to approach this problem was not an official quality improvement team of the hospital, and its members changed as new areas were addressed. Miles initiated and led many of the efforts of the group and was aided by Bingham of MVRMC, Cheryl Juntensen, director of Public Health District V, Maggi Machala, pregnancy program coordinator for Public Health District V, and the ob-gyn physicians in Twin Falls. The group was organized to meet as a whole in making major decisions, but otherwise individuals would carry out their own projects.

In an attempt to clarify the process of prenatal care current at the time, the group tried to use the perspective of the consumer—the patient—to see how the process worked from that viewpoint. Flowcharts were used in attempting to identify obstacles to care. An informal analysis of access to prenatal care was performed by Machala, and a questionnaire was given to mothers who had delivered at MVRMC in an attempt to identify any complaints and concerns they had about their care. Once all of this information was gathered, the group was able to name some areas for improvement. These areas included educating the patient about the hospital before she arrived in labor, improving time delays once in the hospital, and ensuring prenatal care to avoid drop-in deliveries. Within the community, improvement areas focused on access, efficiency, and affordability of care. It was clear to Miles that any efforts at improving the current process could greatly benefit the patient population, but the process of this improvement could be time-consuming and difficult.

As a means of reducing the variation of care within the system, the group tried to identify the main problem areas (Illustration 3.2). With respect to access to prenatal care, multiple factors from financial to psychosocial were impeding the process. In 1988, Medicaid eligibility was set at 43 percent of the federal poverty level, which gave insurance to a small number of people in need. However, even for those who were fortunate enough to receive Medicaid, the reimbursement for prenatal care and delivery was only $400, an amount that did not cover the physician's overhead. Also, from the delivering physician's point of view, many of these patients who could not afford their care were also high-liability concerns with multiple, time-consuming psychosocial issues. The availability of physicians was also a problem. In the area were five obstetricians, located in Twin Falls, with all other deliveries performed by family practitioners. However, if a family practitioner performed more than 40 deliveries per year, then his or her malpractice insurance greatly increased.[11] And so, in an area lacking adequate numbers of physicians, not all patients could receive care, and those cut out of the system were the ones who could not pay or were difficult to manage.

With respect to the efficiency of the system, the obstacles to improvement were identified by Machala.[11] She revealed the difficulty that patients were experiencing because of having to make multiple visits to multiple care sites with numerous delays. A patient making different visits to different sites, for pregnancy testing as well as for Women, Infants, and Children (WIC) and Medicaid reimbursement, would increase the physician-to-patient ratio. Also, the group saw the need to improve the efficiency of clinic visits for the public health patient population. And last, they saw patient education as a necessary component of improving the patient's and community's health while preventing future problems.

Instituting these improvement goals was a long process, and at times different members of the group led the effort. In an attempt to increase the affordability of care by increasing Medicaid eligibility, a group effort was made at the state level to lobby for change. In January

ILLUSTRATION 3.2
Obstacles to Prenatal Care

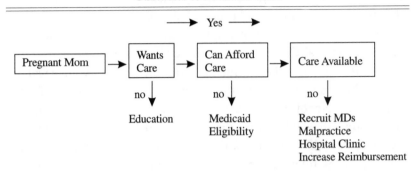

1989, the Medicaid eligibility increased from 43 percent to 67 percent of federal poverty level. In August 1989, the federal Office of Budget Reconciliation Act increased eligibility to 75 percent, and later, in April 1990, the level increased to 133 percent of poverty level.[11] These efforts allowed for many more patients to have insurance and seek care.

However, this increase in Medicaid eligibility did not affect physician reimbursement or physicians' desire to take on new patients. So an eight-member committee, supported by the Idaho Medical Association and the Maternal and Child Health Committee, consisting of obstetricians, family practitioners, and pediatricians, lobbied for a change in the reimbursement policy. By 1990, a change was made that decreased pediatric hospital reimbursement to allow for an increase in obstetrical reimbursement. This effort resulted in an increase of prenatal care and delivery reimbursement from $400 to $1,200.[12]

In the area of improving access to care, MVRMC, the Public Health Department, Family Health Services (a community health clinic), and the obstetricians worked together to ensure availability and efficiency of services. At first, the health department created four decentralized area sites and incorporated "one-stop shopping" at each of these sites.[11] The health department also received a federal Maternal and Child Health grant for all women with income below the 185 percent of poverty level. This block grant ensured comprehensive and efficient prenatal care, including one-stop shopping for pregnancy testing and education, smoking cessation, applying for WIC, Medicaid screening and receipt of a temporary card, nutrition counseling, and social work intervention.

This program expanded services to many women previously uninsured and enabled the patient to be seen promptly by her physician. Timely obstetrical care could now be provided without the physician being concerned with payment or multiple psychosocial issues. Magic Valley Regional Medical Center also established an obstetrical clinic, staffed by the obstetricians in the community, to ensure that any woman wanting care could receive it if she was not able to be seen at a private office.

Another factor of access to care, the low physician-to-patient ratio, has been a problem well known to the people of Idaho, and any previous effort to improve this condition was encouraged again. However, the group was not successful with recruiting efforts, and some of the obstetricians were not willing to make recruitment a priority, concentrating instead on the other improvement areas. However, the family practitioners, who were limited because of malpractice quotas, were soon able to see more patients because the additional malpractice insurance was being paid for by the county hospitals.[11]

In an attempt to improve the patients' education and perceived need for prenatal care, the Public Health Department, through the block grant, began classes, "Baby Your Baby," to educate future mothers about pregnancy, birthing, child rearing, and contraception. The department identified the women who were smoking and tagged their charts so that all healthcare workers could encourage the patients to stop smoking. These women were also enrolled in smoking cessation classes. The health department worked to ensure that all of their patients were thus educated and informed about their healthcare.

From 1988 to 1991 all of these changes were being instituted in an attempt to test the program's hypothesis, and by the end of 1991 the group was ready to begin data analysis and to see if the expected outcome was accurate. The results would help them answer the questions: "How do we know that pregnant women are getting the best prenatal care that they can, and how do we know that the care we give works?"

With respect to affordability, the number of Medicaid deliveries increased dramatically from 123 in 1988 to 231 in 1990, the year reimbursement fees increased to $1,200, and Medicaid eligibility increased to 133 percent of the poverty level. At the same time, the number of drop-in deliveries, those women receiving no prenatal care, declined (Illustration 3.3).

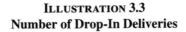

ILLUSTRATION 3.3
Number of Drop-In Deliveries

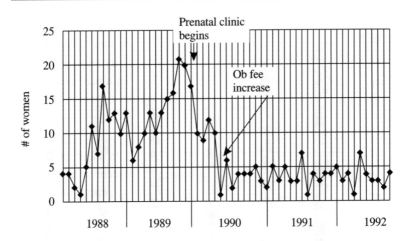

The group also looked at NICU admissions as another indicator of perinatal morbidity, and again they saw a dramatic decline from 184 admissions in 1988 to 137 admissions in 1991. During this decrease in admissions the total number of deliveries at the hospital had increased. The number of NICU patient days, which gives a better indication of how sick the admissions are, showed a steady decline from 1,726 days in 1988 to 974 days in 1990. However, in 1991, the figure increased to 1,162 days. Along with this indicator, low-birthweight figures were analyzed. As hoped for, the incidence of low birth weight decreased along with the increase in prenatal care, but then increased in 1991 (Illustration 3.4).

With respect to patient education, results were not available for review. The Baby Your Baby classes were well attended, but it was difficult to assess the direct effectiveness of these sessions. Similarly, the results of the smoking cessation program are still being studied and follow-up data are being accumulated.

Financially, both increases and decreases occurred in healthcare costs. Because of the expanded eligibility rules, the number of women receiving Medicaid increased. Approximately 200 more women were enrolled, each costing an average of $2,000 per pregnancy. This increase created an additional cost of $400,000. However, along with this increased expenditure for prenatal care came a decrease in NICU patient days.

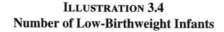

ILLUSTRATION 3.4
Number of Low-Birthweight Infants

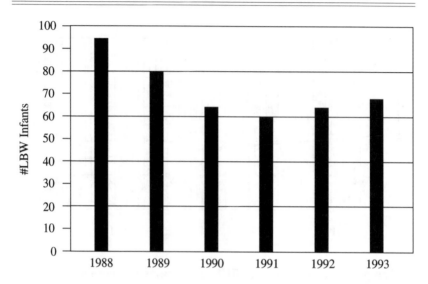

One day in the NICU costs an average of $1,000. In 1988, the total was 1,726 patient days, while in 1990, it decreased to 974 patient days. This change created a savings of $750,000. During 1991, when the total number of days increased to 1,162 days, the savings as compared to 1988 was still $564,000.[12]

Having found these results, the group concluded that their efforts not only had increased the number of pregnant women receiving care but also had improved the health status of their babies, directly contributing to the overall health of the community. The general agreement was to continue the current care they developed, but from their data they were able to identify some problem areas that still needed improvement. One of these areas was the increase in NICU patient days for 1991. Miles was uncertain whether this figure was part of normal variation or something that could be improved. In attempting to explain the NICU data, he discovered that the twinning rate in Twin Falls for that year had increased compared to past years. Twins are at a 50 percent higher risk for low birth weight and at a five times higher risk for mortality than are single births.[10] Miles discovered that in 1991 the twinning rate in the area was double the national average.[8] This increase was most likely the major cause for the increase in NICU patient days.

However, that odd variation of the twinning rate did not satisfy the group. Some members looked at the issue of prenatal care—its definition and implementation. Different aspects of care vary from physician to physician and, interestingly, since 1988 the rate of women beginning prenatal care within the first trimester has been steady at 60 to 63 percent.[1] The significance of this finding is unclear, but the group is curious to see if increasing that percentage could influence perinatal morbidity and mortality.

These areas, along with programs to improve data collection and to make better use of statistics, are some of the projects that are being considered for the group's next improvement undertaking. However, members are also aware of some inevitable roadblocks. One of the other community obstetricians has increased his prenatal care fees to $2,000, which is above the current Medicaid reimbursement amount of $1,200. It is feared that others might follow his move, possibly leading to a significant decrease in affordability and access to care. Also, five family practitioners in Twin Falls are going to stop their obstetrics service. And the hospital clinic closed with the verbal agreement that the obstetricians in town would care for anyone who needed prenatal care—but that outcome has been difficult to track. The Maternal and Child Health Block grant was discontinued in January 1992, leaving many women without access to comprehensive care, and there still remains for all patients a one-month waiting period for the first obstetrical visit. Further, the Hispanic population in the area is growing, but there are no translation services available within the healthcare system. Finally, Medicaid has stated that it will stop all payment from April 1993 to the beginning of its next fiscal year, July 1, 1993. The obstetricians and family practitioners are unsure if they will take on new patients who will be delivering and not paying for their care during the months from April to July 1993.

Miles is concerned about the course that prenatal care could take and would like to readdress the issues of providers, access, and payment as soon as possible. He would also like to have a better understanding of what specific factors in prenatal care truly affect outcome. He has applied for a grant to develop an interactive video to educate future mothers and to develop a systems approach to prenatal care by creating a uniform database and vision within the entire region.[12] However, the views of the group are varied. Juntensen and Machala, in agreement but aware of their decreased funding, continue to follow the health department's pregnancy program annual plan that highlights the community need for prenatal care as well as the strategies to follow in continuing to improve early access and comprehensive care.[13] But because of the anticipated problems for the future of prenatal care, Machala has distributed a pregnancy program progress report (1989–1991) that emphasizes the need to increase the number of women receiving care in the first trimester. There is also concern about the appropriateness of the current content and amount of patient education and whether or not a need exists for specific education before women actually become pregnant. Mr. Bingham continues to support the efforts of the group and the mission of the hospital, but he has become aware that with this initial improvement in the health of the community, the NICU appears to be becoming underused, overstaffed, and less profitable.[7] This financial reality, while not changing Bingham's vision to improve the health of the community, is a factor that is requiring some of his attention. The obstetricians are not interested in recruiting more physicians; they want to see if there is a problem first before making any further efforts to improve prenatal care. The group plans to meet next month to decide what to do next.

Miles has asked Blackwell to plan the agenda for the next meeting and to give him her priority list for the next steps to take. Blackwell knows that Miles expects three questions to be answered: Why do we do what we do, how do we know what we do works, and how can we make what we do better?

Notes

1. Idaho Department of Health and Welfare, *Annual Summary of Vital Statistics* (Boise: IDHW, 1988, 1989, 1990).

2. Conversation with Jodi Craig, August 1992.

3. Magic Valley Regional Medical Center. *MVRMC Current State* (Twin Falls, ID, 1989).

4. M. Walton, *The Deming Management Method* (New York: Putnam Publishing Group, 1986).

5. J. Bronowski, *Science and Human Values* (New York: Harper and Row, Publishers, Inc., 1965).

6. P. M. Senge, *The Fifth Discipline* (New York: Doubleday/Currency, 1990).

7. Conversation with John Bingham, July 1992.

8. Perinatal Data Bank (Magic Valley Regional Medical Center, Twin Falls, ID, 1988).

9. Joint Commission on Accreditation of Healthcare Organizations, *Striving Toward Improvement: Six Hospitals in Search of Quality* (Oakbrook Terrace, IL, 1992).

10. N. F. Hacker and M. Moore, *Essentials of Obstetrics and Gynecology* (Philadelphia, PA: W. B. Saunders Company, 1986).

11. M. Machala and M. Miner, "Piecing Together the Crazy Quilt of Prenatal Care." *Public Health Reports* 106 (July–August 1991): 53–60.

12. P. Miles, *A Systems Approach to Rural Prenatal Care*, Unpublished grant proposal.

13. Idaho Department of Health and Welfare, *Pregnancy Program Annual Plan* (Boise: IDHW, 1992).

Case 4

Reengineering a Physician Practice Utilizing Systems Analysis and Design: Merger and Managed Care Considerations

Joan M. Kiel

Marark Medical Specialists, Inc., located in Texas, is a ten-member physician group that resulted from a merger of four-member and six-member practices. Prior to the merger, the practices had the following characteristics.

The four-member practice, Internal Medical Specialists, Inc., consisted of four board-certified male physicians, three in their upper forties and one in his early sixties. They are in their 22nd year together. The office staffs 21 people: one office manager, Scott Desmond, four full-time registered nurses, six full-time and two part-time medical assistants, one full-time and one part-time front desk personnel, two full-time telephone personnel, three full-time billers and coders, and one full-time file clerk. The practice has 22,700 patients who range from infant to elderly. It is located in a growing suburb north of Dallas.

The six-member practice, Marark Medicine, Inc. (named for the first name initials of its members), consisted of five board-certified physicians, four male and one female, and one board-eligible female physician. They range in age from mid-thirties to mid-fifties. Four have been together for 20 years, with the other two joining ten and four years ago. The office staffs 22 people: one office manager, Janet Hughes, who has just accepted a position at an HMO, three full-time and three part-time nurses, five full-time and two part-time medical assistants, one full-time front desk personnel, two full-time telephone personnel, one manager of information technology, one manager of billing and coding with two part-time billers and coders, and one part-time file clerk. The practice has 34,500 patients who range in age from late teens to the elderly. The practice is located 14 miles west of Dallas.

The merger occurred one month ago as a result of managed care competition and the need for both practices to contain costs. Since Marark Medicine's office manager was leaving, Scott Desmond was made the manager of the merged practices. He has spent his first month in attorney's offices reviewing the merger document and learning the lingo. With such high hopes that this merger will save money and continue to provide quality care, Mr. Desmond has a big job ahead of him.

Scott Desmond is preparing for the first board retreat of the merged practices. His biggest concern is reengineering the information systems (or lack thereof) for efficient and effective operations under managed care. He hopes to institute processes that the merged practice can benefit from without adding pressures to the two staffs that are transitioning their working roles and relationships. To achieve this goal, he will utilize the systems analysis and design process.

Reengineering Information Systems

Prior to the merger of the two practices, Marark Medicine, Inc. had a well-functioning practice management information system (PMIS). This practice had automated scheduling, billing, and electronic medical records. Physicians and staff are well-versed in computer operations and view the PMIS as an important tool to enhance patient care and office operations. Internal Medical Specialists, on the other hand, did not have the advanced systems that Marark did. In fact, their computerization consisted of only four computer terminals utilized for some electronic billing and word processing. They did not view computerization as an important component of the practice management environment. Mr. Desmond needs to examine the issue of information technology in this merged practice. He is going to apply the systems analysis and design process again with the goal of computerization in the next six months.

SYSTEMS ANALYSIS AND DESIGN

The systems analysis and design process has five distinct steps:

1. Analyze the current information systems.
2. Analyze practice processes that are not computerized.
3. Specify information systems needs for the practice.
4. Pilot the information systems.
5. Integrate the information systems into daily operations.

In the first step, Scott sets out to analyze the current information systems by collecting data from physicians, staff, and patients on how the current information systems are contributing to the efficiency and effectiveness of the practice. It appears to be a daunting task at the outset, but Scott decides to jump in by setting up two meetings, the first with the physicians and the second with the staff. These meetings will also get the two practices to meet each other and exchange ideas. He discusses what the user's needs are and what types of systems they are familiar with. During the meetings, he begins to flowchart key systems that utilize information systems such as scheduling and billing. He encourages everyone to get involved with the process. After the staff has completed the flowcharts, he proceeds with the physicians. To his amazement, the physicians outline almost the same flowcharts for the two systems.

Scott also must assess what data is needed by the practice and individual staff members. He gathers this information by meeting with physicians and staff at their work sites—the "walk around management" strategy. What is the format in which people want to see and read the data? He finds that the physicians prefer colorful graphs with less verbiage, but the billers desire to see the entire financial statements in a spreadsheet format. Scott also makes a chart of the frequency of reports needed and by whom. He is analyzing if the present information systems can meet the user's needs.

Last, Scott resorts to his trade journals. Instead of reading the articles, he looks at the advertisements. He is looking for information systems vendors who have products that will meet his users' needs. Advertisements are plentiful, so Scott hangs some on the staff bulletin board to receive feedback. As the first step in the process comes to a close, Scott is confident that he has a list of the advantages and disadvantages of the current system, input from his physicians and staff on their needs, and preliminary vendor information.

Scott then proceeds to the second step of analyzing processes that are done manually. As in the first step, Scott meets with the physicians and staff to garner suggestions for reengineering. These meetings are not as cordial as in the first step. It seems that each practice staff does not want to change the way that they have been doing business. The major area that they cannot agree on is the billing process. Internal Medical Specialists has both manual and automated billing systems, whereas Marark Medicine, Inc. has a computerized system, but it is somewhat dated. Scott knows that this issue will take some time and effort to resolve.

He begins by reverting to the flowcharting process, this time comparing how the process is done manually versus electronically. Scott proceeds with a cost benefit analysis by measuring the time and staff involved and their hourly wages for all steps in the billing process. Although harder to quantify, he also assesses quality and patient satisfaction. Last, he takes an overall picture of how this billing process integrates with the other practice processes. He knows that if the billing is late, the collections will be late, and his budget will not be accurate. It is paramount that this practice be most efficient and effective in their billing processes.

Last, Scott "benchmarks" this practice against others in the area. At his monthly professional meeting of physician office managers, Scott asks his colleagues how they do their billing. He finds that the answers vary by size of practice and revenue. But everyone is telling him that for a merged practice of ten physicians, a manual system will not be efficient. He must reengineer the billing process to include automated systems. At the end of the second step, Scott knows that he will have to change the manual billing process. He begins to think about how the transition will occur and how the change will be received by the merged practice.

The third step involves detailing the specific information systems needs of the practice. Here is where Scott must resolve the billing system issue without ostracizing the staff and damaging the relationships that have been built. In this step, Scott integrates all of the information from the previous two steps, while continuing to involve the physicians and staff in his analysis. He focuses on having the physicians and staff involved in the reengineering process and the selection of the hardware and software. Scott sets up a meeting to discuss the rationale for the new systems and to empower everyone to outline a plan whereby the billing system would be totally converted to an electronic system. At the meeting he tells them that the new, larger practice cannot compete effectively without it. He shows them the results of the reengineering time study comparing one days worth of billing completed electronically versus manually. He begins to win over the staff of Internal Medical Specialists when he outlines new initiatives that can be undertaken because of the saved time. These initiatives involve no overtime or weekend work for billing and include job training in other practice areas such as transcription and coding. Scott is getting positive feedback, but more work must be done.

Scott returns to the vendor advertisements and gets feedback on whom to invite in for a vendor demonstration. The staff decides on three companies: Physician Computing, Inc., Practice Automation, Inc., and Medical Systems Specialists. The vendors each pay a separate visit to the practice. Here they interact with the staff and physicians, the ultimate end users, to assess their needs and wants. The staff and physicians in turn try out the hardware and software. Scott tells them to pay close attention to the ease of use of the products. He does not want to buy an automated system that will only make the billing process more cumbersome. During the visits the physicians and staff are actively engaged with the vendors. Scott is happy to see that they are taking an interest. After the visits, another meeting takes place with everyone to discuss the results. The staff is in favor of Physician Computing, Inc. The physicians cannot decide between them and Practice Automation, Inc. Scott has found that these two companies have similar systems, although Practice Automation, Inc. has more graphical packages that the physicians prefer. Here Scott returns to Physician Computing, Inc. to inquire about adding graphical packages. Although they are not a part of the standard software package, at a cost of $270 for a main copy and $20 per computer site license, Scott can have the graphics and make the physicians and staff happy by selecting Physician Computing, Inc. Scott announces the news of the new system. There is some trepidation, but everyone is happy that they were included in the decision-making process and that their ideas and concerns were considered. At the end of the third step, the practice has decided which system to purchase and the rationale for it.

The fourth step is the make-or-break step, when all of the analysis and design is finally implemented. Here, the new information system is installed and piloted. This change should be implemented when the practice is least busy—perhaps during a summer month or around a holiday. Second, Scott wants to cross-train the staff so that no one person feels solely responsible for the system. Also, if that individual leaves, the practice will have others who can immediately utilize the system. Scott brings the physicians and staff together and reviews what will occur. Training is the key issue. Scott and the vendor will train the two most senior people over a one-week period, including one Sunday when the office is completely closed and total attention can be focused on the new billing system. In turn, the two will train six others over a four-week period. Scott has also budgeted for extra staff to work during the training and for six weeks after so that those working with the new system do not feel as if they have to rush to complete other duties. The vendor will also be available "on call" throughout the training period. Scott also has encouraged the staff to help each other and to rely on the vendor's 24-hour help line.

As the pilot period proceeds, Scott asks for feedback and offers motivation. Staff is becoming familiar and comfortable with the system. Part of the reason is that they were involved from the very beginning— their opinions and expertise were solicited in designing the new system. At the end of this step, the practice should feel comfortable with the new system and begin to see an improvement in efficiency.

The fifth and last step is to integrate the new process into the daily operations. This system will become part of the employee orientation, with the continuing assessment of how the staff, patients, and physicians are working with this new system. Over time, paper bills will no longer be a part of the office and the new electronic system will seem the norm.

Now Scott wants to embody into the management style and office philosophy the ideas of empowering employees to reengineer processes and to continue to assess where improvements can be made. He announces that all routine staff meetings will now include a period of time to brainstorm on practice changes. Employees are encouraged to bring in literature on what other practices are doing or to contribute vendor advertisements. The physicians tell him that they are concerned about budgetary issues, but Scott assures them that ideas will be assessed with the budget in mind. He also tells the physicians that the brainstorming sessions will aim to generate ideas for improvement and cost savings, rather than being a time to complain. At the end of this step, the practice has a working information system and an open philosophy to empower its workers to reengineer the practice to keep it efficient.

Case 5

Organization Design for the Breast Service at Easter Medical Center

Chiara del Monaco
James Paul Volcker

Internal Issues: Background and Unit Organization

Established in early 1992, the breast service seeks to deliver comprehensive care to women with breast disease. The service is a part of the Department of Surgery at Easter Medical Center (EMC), which over the last few years has undergone a wide reorganization focused primarily on information management, operations, employee development, and marketing. The department feels that weaknesses in these areas have stifled its ability to provide quality service and, ultimately, increase market share.

Tangible signs of the reorganization include a restructuring of the Department of Surgery (Illustration 5.1). Physicians have been appointed as vice chairmen for information systems/research, operations/quality management, medical education/employee development, and external affairs. These doctors are responsible to the department chairman for overseeing the redesign of their respective areas. A chief financial officer supervises the business office in the department and provides financial guidance to the vice chairmen and division chiefs in their work. In addition, because physician autonomy and decision making are highly regarded as strengths in the department, a series of division chiefs remain as governors of their respective surgical services. The chiefs provide

Illustration 5.1
Department of Surgery Table of Organization

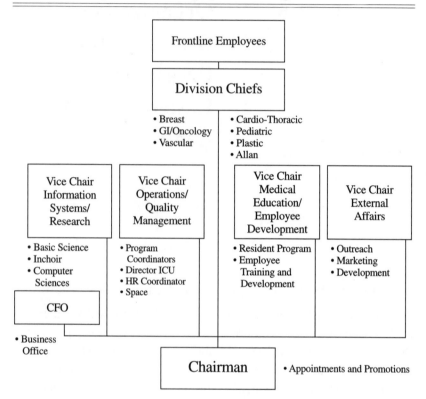

strategic planning within their specific areas and are given discretion to access input from the vice chairs as necessary.

In addition to modifying its hierarchy, the department has created a vision statement and a new "commitment to partnership" (Illustrations 5.2 and 5.3, respectively). The latter document in particular, which includes goals for patient care, has been the impetus for a series of front-line employee workshops to bring about self-awareness and a unified approach to servicing customer needs. In general, departmental leadership has encouraged all employees to voice opinions to improve department service.

It is a strength of the Department of Surgery that it has taken the steps to reorganize as it has. With the advent of managed care, the healthcare industry is no longer "business as usual." Competitive pressures have generated the need for providers to focus not only on delivery of services,

ILLUSTRATION 5.2
Vision

We, the members of the Department of Surgery, are committed to be a continuously improving professional and academic culture dedicated to prolonging and enhancing human life through excellence in clinical practice, teaching, research, and the development of surgical treatment. We will accomplish this by working in close partnership with each other, our patients, and our colleagues throughout the medical center and the larger community.

---

but also increasingly on how those services are delivered. Issues of efficiency within the industry have meant that outcomes assessment has become essential. The contemporary healthcare provider needs to be able to monitor quality of service and have access to data through which to assess outcomes. These new needs have, in turn, required new types of training for the healthcare professional.

The continuance of the division chiefs structure, with the separate surgical services, is a potential weakness of the reorganization. In effect, the surgical fiefdoms remain, governed by the service chiefs. Physician autonomy remains a feature of the department; at best, limited mechanisms of accountability exist within the new structure. Mandating that the surgical services comply with the new way of doing things is nearly impossible—yet it is crucial that the chiefs and the service physicians "buy in" to the reorganization. They have to feel that the changes are positive steps in their work, or the hoped-for improvements will not happen.

Within this context of reorganization, the breast service has tended to maintain the status quo. Nationally and internationally recognized physicians, whose collective reputation bring continuing business to the service via word-of-mouth recommendations, have historically staffed the unit. Within this environment, new technology, competitive pricing, and operating efficiency are not deemed particularly necessary, and the service has largely forfeited opportunities to tap into the new departmental structure for assistance in modernizing operations. Consequently, goals to increase market share, enhance long-term profitability, or meet the needs of physician staff are not actively planned for.

The breast service is also handicapped by its own organizational design. Although physicians on the service report to the division chief,

ILLUSTRATION 5.3
A Commitment to Partnership

We, the members of the Department of Surgery, are committed to providing you, our patients, referring physicians, and colleagues throughout the medical center, with the highest quality service. We will endeavor to do this by holding ourselves to the following standards.

- We will respond to your inquiries and requests promptly, courteously, and thoroughly.
- We will provide you with relevant, comprehensive, and timely information, explanations, and materials.
- We will listen carefully, acknowledge your point of view, and encourage your questions so we may better understand your expectations.
- We will engage you in a collaborative decision-making process to produce the best possible outcome.
- We will work in close partnership with you and use all available resources to solve any problem you might be experiencing.
- We will take the initiative to put you in direct and timely contact with the person who has the knowledge and experience to best serve you.
- We will consistently demonstrate a willingness to meet your needs by going beyond the boundaries of our individual jobs.
- We will treat you with a depth of courtesy that demonstrates dignity, empathy, sensitivity, and utmost respect for the diversity of those we serve.

each operates his or her practice independently. While the advantage of this arrangement is physician autonomy, this delivery design has many weaknesses. The first is high staff costs. Each physician hires between one and three secretaries, whose responsibilities include reception, billing, filing, ordering supplies, and scheduling operations and physician time. In addition, some physicians hire physician extenders (a registered nurse, nurse practitioner, or physician assistant) to provide additional patient care. Little or no cross-futilization of functions exists—tasks are performed and passed on to the next compartment. The second weakness is procedural inefficiency. The senior secretary determines the charges for physician services; these charges are often arbitrary and have no relation to physician effort or practice costs. There is no strategy for the management of supplies/inventory, no standards of documentation for procedures, and mechanism through which to monitor the quality of patient care. Third, the service staff is underdeveloped. Upon hiring, orientation to the EMC is perfunctory at best, and formal training in individual job responsibilities is nonexistent. Office practices are passed along through word-of-mouth, based on "the way we've always done it." The risk of perpetuating errors is therefore great. In 1997, it was discovered that a consistent error by a previous billing secretary had led to a large loss of revenue for one physician practice. The staff does not have a cohesive view of what needs to be done.

Staff development and formalized processes are needed to improve services and reduce mistakes in the breast service. Each office recognizes the need to take such steps, but lacks the necessary time. Heavy clinical responsibilities translate into physicians being, at best, disinterested managers, with all of the ramifications that term implies.

Weaknesses in the organization of the breast service have been exacerbated by a number of changes in physician personnel. Over a recent two-month period, the former service chief resigned and was replaced, one physician terminated her practice, and another has taken an indefinite leave of absence. This staff reduction will represent a significant decrease in service revenues. Two remaining breast surgeons are sharing the financial expenses of the unit. These two physicians have required the assistance of a recent graduate general surgeon to cover the overflow of patients. In addition, of three plastic and reconstructive surgeons integral to the functioning of a comprehensive breast center, one has left, a second plans to leave, and a third is inexperienced. The unit can no longer function independently or comprehensively. The lack of reconstructive surgery undermines the service's stated mission as a comprehensive breast center, forcing patients to go elsewhere for these services.

External Issues: The Response to Change

In addition to internal pressures, the breast service is facing external pressures as well. Under the management of the previous chief, the service did not react to several environmental conditions, which presently makes it less competitive in the local marketplace. Technical changes in the field have been rapidly advancing over the past two years to include a surgical procedure called sentinel lymph node biopsy and the use of the ABBI instrument for surgical treatment of breast cancer. As of yet, however, the breast service has not made a resource commitment in terms of dollars or personnel to these new procedures. Second, the era of information systems technology has been ignored.

The individual physician offices in the service continue to schedule appointments by hand. No integrated system, database collection, or outcomes measurement mechanism exists. Last, the service does not, to date, align itself with any insurance carrier. Provider shifts have taken place within the managed care industry, but the decision not to align endures. Breast service patients who decide to have surgery are informed by the secretary that they are responsible for investigating their own insurance benefits and for paying the remaining balance in its entirety. With the high costs of today's healthcare, many patients are actively seeking competent physicians within provider networks. Breast service physicians believe that the wave of managed care will pass, favoring the traditional fee-for-service model. Although this remains to be seen, it does not mean that care should not be managed efficiently and costs contained. Maintaining a position in the marketplace requires knowing what it costs to care for patients.

Another issue to consider is the reaction of patients to the delivery of care at the breast service. At present, enormous coordinated effort is necessary to take a patient from scheduled appointment to the physician's consultation room, then into the hospital for surgery, and return them home satisfied with the services provided. Within this process are many pockets of inefficiency for staff and patients, resulting in delays and frustration at every point in the process. Historically, most patients have accepted office inefficiencies out of great loyalty to their surgeon. The contemporary woman who seeks care for breast disease has many choices in this marketplace. The question is, will the existing structure remain clinically respected and financially sound amidst the changing internal and external environment? Had the environment remained stable, the breast service might be able to perpetuate its existence with a low level of complexity. This possibility is no longer an option. The breast center must adapt to its environment and upgrade the complexity of its goals, strategy, and structure to maintain viability in the local marketplace. An organization with high complexity is more able to adapt to a changing environment, and adaptability is the key to survival.

Short Case C | CQI at Suburban Hospital

Larry K. McReynolds

Clara Maass Health System is composed of a 475-bed community hospital, a 120-bed long-term facility, a 10-bed subacute unit, and a visiting nurse agency located in north Newark, New Jersey. The hospital is the largest entity of the health system, having been in existence for 125 years. As a community-based nonteaching hospital, the medical staff is an older, conservative group wary of change. The employees pride themselves on being part of their local hospital but have recently become disturbed at the changes occurring in their health system.

The introduction of managed care into the local marketplace has caused the hospital administration much worry that change must occur to service in the immediate future. Some of the key factors causing concern right now are as follows:

1. The county in which Clara Maass is located has 14 other hospitals, making the county overbedded by 200 percent.
2. The competitive environment is enabling managed care companies to force hospitals to take rates below their costs.
3. The hospital's average length of stay and average cost per discharge are significantly higher than those of other hospitals in the area.
4. Many of the physicians are close to retirement and see little reason to change their ways of practicing medicine at this stage of the game.
5. Employee morale is low as a result of cost-cutting, two recent layoffs, and no raise for two years.

Implementation of a CQI program by administration is an attempt to help bring about some of the needed changes in the organization. The hospital CQI program has been approved by the board of trustees and has been in place for almost two years.

Implementation of the CQI program was accomplished through required CQI training for managers, all employees, and as many physicians as possible. Initially, quality action teams (QATs) were chartered to examine clinical and operational issues. The patient services department selected the CareMap format for addressing physician and multidisciplinary issues. CareMaps are multidisciplinary tools for establishing protocols, outcomes, and length of stay.

CareMaps were developed using the primary nurse model placing the nurse as the responsible party for keeping the patient on the map. Operational QATs were chartered by the steering committee to address processes and procedures that were high-volume, problem-prone, costly, or likely to have an adverse effect on the patient. Elements predictive of patient satisfaction were also used to determine if a QAT should be chartered.

To facilitate integration of CQI principles among all employees, managers attend an ongoing workshop. This monthly meeting is designed to provide a nonthreatening forum for managers to examine their department processes and outcomes and the degree of the department's success in meeting the customer's needs. Ideas from the workshop and suggestions from the CareMap and QATs are approved by the steering committee and implemented by the team.

Case Questions

1. Employees have the feeling that eliminating "wasted work" and improving processes is a fancy way of eliminating more jobs. Identify strategies to overcome this impression.
2. Managers feel this is the management philosophy of the week. Identify and describe effective means to overcome this barrier.
3. Physicians see CareMaps as cookbook medicine imposed upon them by the nursing department. Describe ways to get them to "buy-into" CareMaps.
4. Identify organizational strategies that the hospital should adopt to make the institution more viable in the marketplace.

Short Case D | ER at Queens Hospital Center

Anthony R. Kovner

Currently 83 percent of patients at the Queens Hospital Center emergency room are treated and released. They wait six to eight hours for treatment. The goal is to decrease waiting time and the number of walkouts and to improve care and patient satisfaction.

Current Procedure:

Step 1. Patient seen by triage nurse.

Step 2. Patient sent to registration.

Step 3. Patient waits to be seen by physician.

Step 4. Patient sent for any necessary lab or x-ray.

Step 5. Patient waits for test results to be reviewed by MD.

Step 6. Patient treated, discharged, or admitted.

Case Question

1. What do you suggest to improve the process? To reduce errors by the triage nurse?

Short Case E | Sparks Medical Center and the Board of Trustees

Anthony R. Kovner

Sam Phillips, chairman of Sparks Medical Center's board of trustees, wondered why hospital board meetings were so different from those at his spice company, Phillips' Flavors, Inc. The hospital board discussed the reports of various committees, reviewed accreditation and licensing reports, and listened to reports and recommendations about state regulations and reimbursement. At Phillips' Flavors, Inc., the board discussed the future of business, what the competition was doing, and strategies to increase market share and profit margins.

Clara Burns, CEO of Sparks Medical Center, made the following recommendations to Sam Phillips regarding more effective board meetings:

1. Board discussion should focus on the organization's mission.
2. Objectives and strategies should be established.
3. A work plan to plan and measure board performance should be developed.

Sam realized that the problem with addressing these issues was the board structure and organization and the amount of time taken up at meetings by routine committee and management reports. This resulted in a full agenda and little time to deal with issues critical to the future of the Medical Center.

Case Questions

1. What do you recommend that Sam do now?
2. Identify constraints and opportunities that Sam faces in implementing your recommendations.

Part III

Organizational Design

Introduction

In healthcare, discussion about organizational design occurs at four levels. The first is at the patient care level under capitation and managed care. New questions are being asked. How do we organize the best care for asthma or hypertension or back pain? Answering this question requires a definition of "best," data on the population served, a team of staff members working to achieve these goals, and management support. How does our organization answer these questions? What is excellent diabetes care? How would we know we are achieving it?

At the next level of aggregation are the issues of the design of the hospital, nursing home, and other care organizations. How do we put the component departments together? Restructuring, reengineering, and downsizing are the jargon terms of the moment. The Wise Medical Center case raises some of these issues, as does the VNA of Cleveland case.

Across the country, hospitals, clinics, and insurers are grouping themselves together as systems of care. In an urban area where 30 separate hospitals once stood, there may now be four competing groups of hospitals. These may be nonprofit organizations, investor-owned such as Columbia HCA, or a mix of both. This new grouping strategy is the third level of organizational design.

One reason for these changes is the recognition that with managed care we will need many fewer hospital beds than we now have. The leaders of a single hospital left out of such a system may well wonder if they will be one of the hospitals that will disappear. One way these mergers are occurring is through the sale of a nonprofit hospital to a for-profit group. The sale price plus the nonprofit hospital's existing endowment is put into a nonprofit foundation. The income from this foundation's endowment is used to achieve the charitable and philanthropic goals of the original nonprofit hospital. The hospital, now part of the for-profit organization, will be run along business lines in a very competitive environment.

In the rush to become one of the three or four biggest groups in the area, the system bases its decisions about organizational design on expediency, comfort level, and speed rather than organizing to provide expeditious, excellent care. The local rush for size is of vital importance in a market oversupplied with hospitals. Any one urban hospital priced too high or of average quality can be ignored by a managed care system. For such a hospital to exist, it will have to accept whatever price the managed care systems choose to offer, which will not be high. If the system is large enough and includes popular, specialized, and prestigious hospitals, then all managed care systems or insurers must deal with them. Such a system will not be a "price taker" but a "price giver." It can charge a full price for its services because the HMO or insurer has no choice.

The fourth level is at the state- or national-policy level. The most notable effort in the last few years to change the context of healthcare delivery was the Clinton administration's unsuccessful national health plan initiative.

The current devolution of decision making related to Medicaid from the federal to the state level will also change the context of care. Some states such as Hawaii and Oregon are providing interesting examples of system reform.

It is the interaction of all four of these levels of organization and system design that makes healthcare delivery a most lively arena. The field is creating unprecedented opportunities for creative leadership and the organization of whole new ways of providing better care at lower cost.

The Cases

The coordination of many different professional workers with varying skills, views of the world, perceptions of what needs to be done, and licensing statutes lies at the heart of this new design for health services organizations.

Work can be organized in many different ways in large health services organizations: by task or purpose, by facility, or by client group served. Often, several different organizing principles operate in the same organization, sometimes appropriately and sometimes for historical reasons. As Clibbon and Sachs have pointed out, a laboratory is a place, obstetrics is a health condition, outpatients are people, dietary is a service, intensive care is a need, day care is a category of residential status, radiology is a group of techniques, and rehabilitation is a purpose.[1]

The structure of many healthcare organizations was more appropriate for conditions when the organization was founded than it is for today. Organization structure is determined in part by the nature of the work the organization has to do, its physical facilities, the history of the organization, and the culture of the society and of like institutions.

As academic health centers respond to competitive pressures, their organizational structures may have to be adapted for optimum organizational survival and growth. Sam Spellman has devised an ambitious reorganization plan for Wise Medical Center. What would happen if nothing is done and the current organizational structure is retained? What are the costs and benefits of Spellman's proposal? What are the problems and constraints Spellman faces in implementing his proposal? If the new methods for organizing make so much sense, why aren't other academic health centers already implementing them?

The Betterman Memorial Hospital case describes the unintended consequences of the corporate reorganization of a small rural hospital. Changing the organization structure created new, dysfunctional human relations. Once such conflicts start, they are not easily reversed.

The concept of "disease management" tries to answer the question "How do we organize the best care for a defined population with this condition?" Under capitation this needs to be done in a manner that gives value for money. Combine this with the growing use of the Internet, and disease-related voluntary societies like the American Heart Association or the Special Disease Society may have new roles they could play in partnership with managed care organizations.

Case Questions

Proposal for the Restructuring of Wise Medical Center

1. What are the arguments for and against restructuring?
2. What are the preconditions necessary to allow such restructuring to take place?
3. What are the key obstacles to restructuring?
4. How can these obstacles be overcome?
5. What do you advise Sam Spellman to do? Why?

The Corporate Reorganization of Betterman Memorial Hospital

1. What do you suggest should have been done differently when corporate reorganization was first considered?
2. What do you recommend the administrator do now?

Special Disease Society of America

1. How should Deborah rewrite this plan?
2. What kind of skills are needed to carry out this plan?
3. Does the arthritis disease management program have relevance to the society?
4. What advice would you give about developing their web site? (You might wish to visit several web sites to see what other disease-focused voluntary societies are doing.)

Note

1. Sheila Clibbon and Marvin L. Sachs, "Health Care Facilities: An Alternative to Bailiwick Planning in Patient Fostering Spaces," *The New Physician* 18 (June 1969): 462–471.

Selected Bibliography

Burns, Lawton R., and Darrell P. Thorpe. "Trends and Models in Physician-Hospital Organization." *Health Care Management Review* 18, no. 4 (1993): 7–20.

Griffith, John R. *The Well-Managed Health Care Organization*, 4th Edition. Chicago: Health Administration Press, 1999, Chapter 5.

Herzlinger, R. E. "The Managerial Revolution in the U.S. Health Care Sector: Lessons from the U.S. Economy." *Health Care Management Review* 23, no. 3 (1998): 19–29.

Lathrop, J. P. "The Patient-Focused Hospital." *Healthcare Forum Journal* 34, no. 4 (1991): 16–21.

Leatt, P., S. M. Shortell, and J. R. Kimberly. "Organization Design," in S. Shortell and A. Kaluzney, eds., *Health Care Management: Organization Design and Behavior*, 4th Edition, Albany, NY: Delmar Publishers, 2000, pp. 274–306.

McDonagh, K. J. (ed.). *Patient-Centered Hospital Care: Reform from Within*. Chicago: Health Administration Press, 1993.

Shortell, S. M. "The Future of Hospital-Physician Relationships. Revisiting the Garden: Medicine and Management in the 1990s." *Frontiers of Health Services Management* 7, no. 1 (fall 1990): 3–32.

Case 6 | A Proposal for the Restructuring of Wise Medical Center

Anthony R. Kovner
Louis Liebhaber

This proposal is written by Sam Spellman, chief operating officer, to stimulate a discussion regarding the future structure of a 700-bed hospital in a large Midwestern city.

Wise Medical Center (WMC) faces the enormous challenge of delivering healthcare services in an external environment whose only hallmarks are chaos and change. Issues of an unprecedented nature confront us and will continue to do so at an increasingly rapid pace with increasingly higher stakes.

   Some examples of these issues include:

- epidemics of AIDS, TB, drug abuse, and mental illness;
- overnight shifts in surgical techniques, such as laparoscopy, that will continue to burgeon;
- significant shifts from inpatient to ambulatory surgery;
- provider shifts such as a major pending penetration of managed care into the urban market;
- tremendous momentum for a significant change in the financing of healthcare;
- regulatory and marketplace controls to support the new financing options;
- greater consumer involvement in treatment decisions;

- biotechnological treatments for diseases, resulting in a variety of dislocations: medical versus surgical treatment of an increasing number of diseases; earlier detection of some diseases; extraordinarily expensive treatment, etc.;
- unprecedented competition among various sectors—hospitals, for-profit niche companies, outpatient options, and physicians;
- state drive for capitation of Medicaid in two years; and
- increasingly expensive—possibly rationed—technology.

In the face of these challenges, and those as yet uncontemplated, the question is: *Will the existing organizational structure of an acute care teaching hospital provide enough agility, adaptability, and swiftness to maintain or surpass its current position in the marketplace (financially sound, clinically respected, etc.)?*

Lessons from other sectors of the economy would provide us with a resounding word of caution against complacency toward the shape of our organization.

- Fully half of the *Fortune* 500 companies that were on the *Fortune* 500 list in 1980 were no longer on that list in 1990.
- To avoid sliding farther into an abyss, IBM recently split itself into 13 separate companies.
- AT&T split into multiple companies and is now more successful than at any time in its history.
- GM fell asleep and lost unprecedented BILLIONS of dollars while other new entries to that heavy industry were making unprecedented profits.
- Major teaching hospitals in our city have lost millions of dollars in the past several years.

Multiple lessons can be learned from what is happening in the world around us. We should examine that world and at least discuss and think through ways for us to adapt to it so that we can remain successful into the future. Below I have set out some thoughts whose origins come from many places, including thoughts and discussion that have already begun to surface at WMC. I offer the scenario below as a jumping-off point for discussion and development, not as a complete prescription for the future.

What are the organizational key concepts to WMC's future given the premise of unprecedented continual change?

How can an organization such as WMC anticipate change, adjust course, refocus resources and staff, and achieve equilibrium until the next change that must be anticipated and addressed?

I would argue that one response to this question is to redesign our organization into a manageable number of smaller, more autonomous business entities. These smaller entities (described in detail below) would be organized around the major current businesses of WMC. They would have a degree of autonomy that would facilitate decision making, respond to the environment, and, most important, foster a far greater sense of commitment and purpose to each entity. Such autonomy—with clear accountability—would foster a passionate focus while at the same time adding synergy to the whole. The organization that would evolve would be flatter, more responsive and accountable, much more agile, and cost-effective.

WMC would be divided into at least the following businesses, all linked to the whole through a set of accountabilities and organizational structure and support. There must clearly be a balance, however, recognizing that the success of the whole is more dependent on the success of the individual pieces than in the current structure.

The businesses would be:

- *The Surgical Hospital* (to include all surgical services including the ORs, endoscopy, ambulatory, surgery, etc.)
- *The Private Attending Medical Hospital* (an expansion of what we now call AOS—with the added involvement of the private attendings in the management and definition of the unit)
- *The General Medical Hospital* (the medicine and nonsurgical teaching service)
- *The Maternal and Child Health Hospital* (pediatrics and obstetrics)
- *Ambulatory Care Business* (to include clinics, managed care, and faculty practice)
- *Psychiatric and Substance Abuse Hospital*
- *Rehabilitation Institute*
- *Alternative Site Corporation* (dialysis, home care, and other)
- *Clinical Support Entities* (radiology, lab, cardiology, etc.)

- *Corporate Services*—with potentially several subcompanies (to include food services, housekeeping, security, training, human resources, information systems, etc.)

All of the entities above were given titles that are intended to identify not only the activities and functions that are included, but also to distinguish them as major lines of business; hence, the word "division" is not used, but the word hospital is—to signify a high degree of autonomy and scope.

Each of the major entities would be led by a COO or jointly led by a high-level administrative leader and physician. These leaders would be charged with the integrity, bottom-line performance, quality assurance, development, and implementation of a set of strategic and long-range objectives, and each would be accountable to the central management of WMC.

Each entity would have a specific focus. Some are obviously direct providers of patient care. In that role they are charged with developing and growing their piece of the WMC business. Because the management is clearly focused and is responsible for a relatively manageable-sized entity, where all of the employees and medical staff can actually know each other and where a clear ethic, purpose, and accountability can be established, the likelihood of success in meeting the needs of customers and in anticipating and reacting to the environment should be greatly enhanced.

Following is a detailed description of such an entity.

THE SURGICAL HOSPITAL

The leadership would focus on the present and future environment for surgery. What are the trends? What are the threats and opportunities? What are the needs of our current and potential customers? How do we organize, refocus, communicate, and operationalize the necessary response? Take any specific example—let's say laparoscopic surgery. The surgical hospital leadership would be expected to understand and anticipate the implications of laparoscopic surgical growth and change; confer with its constituents (the surgeons of various specialties); develop a business approach to the issue, which might include a plan for acquiring equipment, training skilled technical staff, regearing the ORs for the technology, providing a marketing plan to HMOs for LOS reduction, and so on. The changing focus, which might also include redirecting resources on the inpatient side, could be communicated to all of the staff in the surgical hospital so that they could in turn prepare for and contribute to the successful implementation of the change.

The proposed reorganization differs from the current environment in several important ways:

- Management of our major businesses would be focused specifically on those businesses. The success of those businesses would also be clearly focused on defined individuals with defined resources.
- The size of the entity would be such that the management can communicate effectively with all of the players: the more rapid the need to change, and the more profound the changes that might occur, the greater the need for meaningful, comprehensive buy-in and communication. That communication is infinitely more likely to succeed in an organization one can touch and feel, and also in an organization with which the players can much more closely identify.
- Each entity would be less captive to the bureaucracy and more focused on its mission and customers.
- Each entity, because of its focus and size, increases the likelihood of harnessing the potential of our CQI effort and the potential power of the human imagination and the creativity of our workforce.
- These entities are much more likely to operate with a higher degree of internal accountability and consistency. Innovation can be introduced and can take hold much more successfully.
- The new entities will have fewer layers in their organization structure, resulting in lower cost, greater agility, and more resources focused on the end result.
- As described below, the entities become discerning purchasers of service rather than part of the structure that may limit the positive effects of competition and innovation.

If one looks at some of the more successful and market-sensitive (defined as agile and cutting edge) entities in WMC, they are relatively self-contained units managed by a focused group of people with a well-defined mission: *hospice, rehab, dialysis, stuy square, the long-term care division* (and even specific inpatient units such as substance abuse, MICU, SICU, etc.).

For an example of a functional entity as opposed to a direct business entity, let's take a look at *corporate services*:

Corporate services comprises those nonclinical functions that support the direct delivery of our main services (patient care). Corporate services are functions such as billing, housekeeping, food service, security, MIS, marketing, human resources, and so forth. Under the proposed plan, they would function much like subcontractors to provide service to the delivery arm, and be held to a standard of performance that one would expect in the competitive world of subcontracting. If the subcontractor for food service, for example, could not demonstrate that it was providing a market-competitive product at a market-competitive price, then the service entity would have the option to subcontract out that service. Even if we were ultimately constrained from actually doing so, the perceived possibility might drive innovation and improvement on the part of the management and workers of food service.

In this scheme every service, almost without exception, could be viewed as a subcontractor with the potential to be replaced by a competitor. The only service that probably would not be subjected to this provision is MIS—and that is only because of the constant state of development in which we find ourselves. It is not inconceivable that we could hire a service bureau and contract out most of MIS also. Even billing could be subjected to a "show me" scenario.

Clearly subcontracting has pitfalls but they may be seriously counterbalanced by the competitiveness, innovation, cost reduction, and flexibility this approach could engender. Further, if our services were so far superior, we could do as we have in food service, and the food service function could seek to provide services on a for-profit basis to other hospitals or businesses.

The *raison d'etre* of corporate services (as with the other functional support entity, clinical support) is to provide responsive, cost-efficient support to the main business entities of WMC. Corporate and clinical services would provide the services and expertise that would not necessarily be economically feasible to subdivide in each business entity, and the provision of which would simply encumber or side-track the efforts of the management of the business entity with tasks that were a tangential, albeit a necessary, part of their business.

The Flatter Organization

The organization described above becomes flatter than the current organization in several ways.

First, each direct care delivery entity—for example, the private attending medical hospital—is of a manageable size (approximately 150 to 225 beds, 400 to 600 employees). All of the direct service providers and subcontractors are accountable to the COO of each entity. Each patient care unit within the entity would have a highly skilled nurse manager and/or head clinician and administrative type (although the latter structure may be less appealing). All of the staff who worked on the unit would be directly accountable to the unit leadership (akin to the Planetree model, although this proposal goes several steps further). The unit managers (whether nurse or some combination) report directly to the COO; with only five to ten units (maximum size), this should be possible.

Second, there would be a natural imperative in this unit-based scenario to innovate and redefine some unit-based jobs to run more smoothly and cohesively—that is, possibly combining patient-focused jobs such as housekeeping, food service, and nurses aide functions.

Third, given the competitive subcontractor model described above, it will be impossible for many services to be market-competitive with the bureaucracy and layering currently in place. These layers are a part of the current fabric and cannot easily be replaced without a different sort of organization to serve.

I am not sure if it is possible to enter into this sort of organizational restructuring on a "pilot" basis, simply because it is so contrary to the current organizational structure. There is far too much potential for undermining, confusion, and waste if there are two parallel tracks exists.

Sam Spellman convened a meeting of top managers to discuss his proposal for restructuring WMC. These included Paul Bones, chief of medicine; Pam Ewing, vice president for nursing; Tom Starks, director of human services; Tony Rivers, vice president for finance; Lew Oakley, director of planning; and Carl Smith, the WMC CEO. A summary of highlights from their discussion follows:

Tony Rivers: Don't we have enough on our minds without drastically reorganizing patient care services? We should be focusing our energies on organizing for managed care rather than on the internal production of services.

Paul Bones: How are we going to factor in our teaching and research objectives and strategies? We should be paying more attention to teaching and research, since this is what makes us distinctive as a hospital.

Pam Ewing: Where does nursing service figure in all this restructuring? It looks to me as if we would be losing a lot of power with no guarantee that services would be better or cheaper. You're going to put the doctors in charge of the nurses, and I'm not so sure that they ought to be telling us what to do or how we can best work together.

Tom Starks: How are you going to bring the unions into this kind of restructuring?

Lew Oakley: Are you suggesting that we could start contracting out a service like our planning department? Wouldn't there be tremendous costs in developing and evaluating different proposals, plus a lot of uncertainty created among my staff, who are doing the best possible job that they know how to do?

Carl Smith: Sam, I think your scheme is a great idea, and I think the people at Hopkins and elsewhere have carried it out with some pretty impressive results. What worries me is that (1) only a few places nationally have gone into this, and the expenditures in training and planning and executive attention would be very great at a time when we're under a lot of pressure to lower our costs; (2) where are WMC's champions to fight for development and implementation of this imaginative proposal? and (3) do our chiefs really have the skills and experience necessary to run these divisions? We didn't recruit them because they were excellent managers, but rather because of their leadership capabilities to run first-rate teaching programs and stimulate the production of research within their specialty.

Case 7 | The Corporate Reorganization of Betterman Hospital

Duncan Neuhauser

Betterman Memorial Hospital is a not-for-profit, 25-bed community general hospital in a small rural town in a predominantly rural state. By 1980, the hospital had accumulated an endowment of $3 million, largely from gifts from a few wealthy families. Betterman considered itself quite fortunate, until its state, responding to the problems of rising healthcare costs, empowered the State Insurance Commission to review and define hospital reimbursement. The State Insurance Commission proposed to deduct at least the interest on Betterman's endowment from revenues the hospital would receive from third-party payers, thus making these assets worthless to the hospital. It was even rumored that some commission hotheads wanted to eliminate all reimbursement to the hospital until the $3 million endowment was entirely used up.

To avert these threats to the endowment, the hospital rushed through a corporate reorganization, going from a single corporation to three (see Illustration 7.1).

The Corporate Structure

The *incorporators,* numbering about 250 people, live in the area and vote approval for new members. They meet once a year (about 50 incorporators attend) to hear an upbeat report on the hospital, vote for new incorporators, and endorse the slate of trustees of the foundation, proposed by the nominating committee of the foundation trustees.

The not-for-profit *foundation* holds the endowment assets, and its trustees meet monthly with the administrator and chief financial officer.

In this small organization, these two administrators manage all three organizations. The hospital itself is the largest part and consumes most of their time. The foundation trustees approve board members for the two other corporations for three years at a time. These terms are renewable and appointments are staggered.

The *for-profit* subsidiary is a small undertaking that generates revenues, one-fiftieth of what the hospital does. Any profits this subsidiary makes go to the foundation. The *not-for-profit* Betterman Hospital and its board are involved in the direct management of the hospital. Its board meets monthly or more often, as needed. The administrators and chief financial officer staff and meet with all three boards.

Corporate Interrelationships

The three corporate boards do not overlap and they meet separately. This independence was created on advice of counsel to ensure separation and thereby protect the endowment assets. In addition, the foundation is to spend at least 10 percent of its endowment income on projects independent of the hospital. These funded proposals have included support for the regional volunteer ambulance corps, a retirement community, and an ambulatory care center at the periphery of the hospital's service area. Approximately 90 percent of the endowment income goes to the hospital for specific projects or to meet operating deficits.

Although the boards did not meet together, their minutes were shared and, as in any small town, members often knew each other and met outside the hospital.

For several years, this arrangement and corporate structure worked well, but with time the roles of the three boards became increasingly unclear:

Foundation Trustee: I see us as the corporate headquarters and the other organizations as subsidiaries.

Hospital Board Member: We run the hospital; we have a direct working knowledge of the hospital, while the foundation board does not. Their role is to manage the endowment assets and turn the interest over to us. That endowment was given to help the hospital.

For-Profit Board Member: At the moment we are a very small activity: we run a home health agency that breaks even. Our charter is to make money for the foundation and the hospital, but our home care agency provides a useful community service and should be continued, even if it does not make money. We also put on a statewide health conference, hoping to make a profit from it. However, we lost money and had to be reimbursed by the foundation, but that was before I was on this board.

Foundation Board Member: We see one of our roles as raising money for the hospital. However, no one knows our corporate name (The Regional Health Foundation) and they write checks to "Betterman Hospital" and the money goes to the hospital directly and is used for working capital. We also are empowered by the bylaws to do long-range planning. However, we have done little of that; we tend to respond to specific proposals for funds as they come to us.

New Problems

Last year the hospital board minutes reflected several important issues. A new contract with the physicians for emergency coverage, office space, and billing was being negotiated. A computer foul-up delayed billing for the hospital, creating a large negative debt. The hospital's cash position was supported by the sale of a gift to the hospital of a piece of property for $300,000, which was put into working capital. The national nursing shortage was felt locally, leading the hospital to approve a one-time large jump in nursing salaries and benefits. Although this would cause a deficit for the year after the outstanding bills were collected, the hospital board told the nurses that they would seek or receive (the exact message remains unclear) money from the foundation to pay for this. The foundation trustees, after reading the hospital board minutes, came to the conclusion that the hospital was having serious problems, and they wanted an explanation.

First Foundation Trustee: The $300,000 should have come to the foundation and not stayed in the hospital. We would probably have added it to our endowment or loaned it to the hospital.

Second Foundation Trustee: We are responsible to the incorporators to be sure that our subsidiary corporations are being well managed.

Third Foundation Trustee: The hospital presented us with a demand for money to pay the nurses. They were making our decisions for us, when we are supposed to tell them what to do. We did not approve their request right away, but said we would think about it.

First Hospital Board Member: We explained in writing that the computer problem was temporary and being resolved. We think we are running the hospital responsibly. The foundation wants to meddle in hospital affairs with which they are not familiar.

Second Hospital Board Member: The foundation's problem is that they have nothing to do. Their endowment is managed by a Chicago bank. People originally gave that money to help the hospital. All the foundation should do is turn the interest over to the hospital. It's as simple as that.

Foundation Trustee: When we tabled the proposal for nurses' pay pending further discussion, the hospital board told the nurses that we refused their agreed-upon request for a pay raise. This makes us look like the bad guys and is irresponsible of the hospital board. They can promise anything, if someone else (that is us) pays for it.

The nurses invited the foundation trustee chairman to meet with them. He did so, explained the foundation's view, and obliquely implied that the hospital was being mismanaged. When the administrator and the hospital board chairman heard about this they were very upset. The hospital chairman wrote a letter to the foundation chairman saying that it was discourteous of him not to notify the hospital board about the meeting with the nurses and implying that it would be better if he stayed out of the hospital's affairs.

The Bylaws

The long-ignored bylaws of the three corporations—written in a rush in 1980—were brought out, dusted off, reproduced for the trustees and board members, and carefully read by all of them (mostly for the first time). However, the only thing the bylaws revealed was substantial ambiguity or complete silence on the several boards' responsibilities.

Two separate law firms were retained by the hospital and the foundation to interpret these bylaws. The foundation's lawyers said that the original distance between the corporations was no longer necessary. The hospital's lawyers urged that the distance be kept. The foundation chairman wrote to the hospital board chairman asking for a joint meeting of the two boards based on this advice. The hospital chairman refused to meet on the basis of their legal advice. A close reading of the several bylaws showed that any important interpretation or corporate change could be argued in court for a long (and expensive) time with the outcome unclear.

Except for the process of appointing trustees, the bylaws gave no advice about the relative roles of the corporations. Probably each corporation could change its own bylaws, but this was arguable.

Administrator: I would like this problem resolved, I sincerely would. It is taking up a lot of my time and staff time, which could be better spent elsewhere. The division of activity between the corporations could be made in a lot of different ways, and I could live with any one of them as long as there is agreement. I try to stay neutral and helpful, but it is difficult. Even so, depending on who wins this power struggle, my job is at risk. In a small town like this, these conflicts don't stay hidden long and become public knowledge, which would do us no good. I wish I knew how to resolve this.

ILLUSTRATION 7.1
Betterman Memorial Hospital Corporate Structure
Before and After 1980

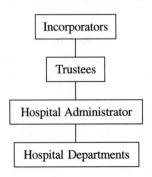

After 1980 and Corporate Reorganization

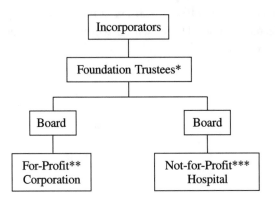

*The Regional Health Foundation, not-for-profit.
**The Regional Health Corporate Ventures, for-profit.
***Betterman Memorial Hospital, not-for-profit.

Case 8 | Special Disease Society of America

Myron Day
Robin Borchardt

Deborah Lovecky, director of communications, marketing, education and advocacy, presents her plans for the coming year to a subcommittee of the society's board, March 1999. Present are three board members: Ann S., Steven K., and the CEO, Sarah N.

Thank you for giving me this opportunity to advise you on how the communications unit in our department should be reorganized to better serve our constituents. Revising our structure will not only aid us in reaching the goals and objectives set by the board of trustees and the national executive director/CEO, but will also ensure that we effectively provide high-quality programs and services for our client-members located across the country. According to the 1998–99 Plan of Work, our department has been charged with the task of "raising $125,000 in support of SDSA's financial goals and to implement and manage a national promotional and public relations program." Ten specific objectives have been identified to the entire unit for realization of these goals. They include the following:

- developing three issues of *The Marker;*
- producing 12 issues of *Happenings;*
- producing the 1998 annual report by April 1, 1999;
- redesigning SDSA's web site to focus more on fundraising;
- coordinating public relations and promotional aspects of SDSA's programs;
- producing two issues of *Toward a Cure;*

- expanding the current awareness campaign, "Give a Voice to SD," to more locales across the country;
- facilitating, monitoring, and evaluating media coverage of SD and SDSA;
- developing a strategic marketing plan to access and prioritize SDSA's overall communication needs; and
- developing more educational products/resources.

As you know, since the writing of the FY99 Plan of Work, SDSA has reorganized the operations at the national office with the intent of better positioning the organization to more adequately respond to the needs of the Special Disease (SD) community. Because our department is charged with overseeing all of SDSA's communication, marketing, education, and advocacy activities, we spend a substantial time interacting with the public. The communications unit experiences our most crucial interactions with SDSA's client members through the publications they produce: *The Marker, Toward a Cure, Caregiver's Link,* and *SDKIDS.* Our department is evaluated on its ability to meet the objectives set forth by the board of trustees and the national executive director/CEO, which makes it imperative that we operate from a client-focused perspective. The needs of people affected by SD should come before the organization's needs for survival and growth. Basically, there is no reason for SDSA's existence (or our department's existence) if our client members feel that we are not working to fulfill their needs.

Currently, our department is organized in a traditional hierarchical structure that manages from the top down, assigns work to unit members in a haphazard fashion, and focuses on individualism and competition. Illustration 8.1 specifies how work is currently organized in our department. This organizational design has allowed SDSA to achieve most of its goals and objectives in the past. First, it is easier to attract potential employees because discrete sets of skills are required of job applicants and performance evaluations are directly related to their competencies with these skills. Second, each department employee is accountable for clear and specific activities, which benefits the organization as less training is required resulting in lower costs. Third, employees are easier to retain because less time is required for training commitments.

ILLUSTRATION 8.1
Current Organizational Design

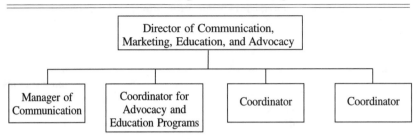

Although the current organizational design contains the aforementioned strengths, this structure has notable weaknesses that have amplified as our organization has expanded. For instance, last year, SDSA's annual operating budget was approximately $1 million. This year, the organization is expected to raise more than $5 million that will be funneled immediately into new programs and expanded services. The organization will need different types of people to manage our ballooning resources and new activities. The new positions we create must be staffed by people with new competencies, skills, and the desire to continually increase their knowledge, skills, abilities, and other characteristics (KSAOCs) necessary to successfully perform their work. The current organizational design discourages the type of workers that we will need in the future from applying to positions at SDSA because of our current rigid, traditional structure that fails to promote risk-taking and/or initiative-taking. Also, SDSA can no longer fail to invest in its employees. Today it is too costly to simply hire new employees when existing workers lack the ability to meet organizational goals. A better way must exist.

Based on my experience with SDSA and our leadership's current plans for future development of the organization, we propose a new organizational design for our department (see Illustration 8.2). The benefit of the proposed organizational design is that it minimizes the weaknesses of the current organizational design, maximizes the current design's strengths, and introduces new strengths in response to changing trends in the healthcare industry. The new organizational design requires that our department's staff function as project managers who rotate

ILLUSTRATION 8.2
Proposed Organizational Design for Department of
Communications, Marketing, Education, and Advocacy

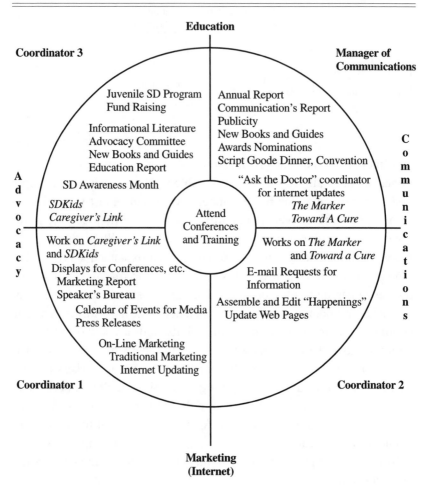

projects, which enables each person's performance to be compared to one another. The strength of this approach is that it allows department employees to eventually develop the KSAOCs necessary for success in every aspect of our department. This cross-functional learning, in and of itself, should motivate new professionals who recognize that product management design structures are one of the latest trends of our industry, a direct result of the managed care movement. The possible weakness of this approach is that it could foster competition among staff members within our department. However, we could overcome this threat by using peer evaluations as one aspect of annual employee performance appraisals. Evaluation criteria such as teamwork and cooperation should be included in this process.

The current organizational design segregates fiscal management and program management responsibilities. Specifically, the accounting department is responsible for the fiscal oversight of all our organization's activities, which include program financing. The proposed organizational design would hold project managers accountable for the fiscal management of programs under their control. No longer would project managers rely on resources from unrestricted donations to finance their operations once they expend the funds in their project budgets. Furthermore, one aspect of project managers' performance evaluations should be based on their ability to control costs associated with their programs.

The strength of this approach is that it makes project managers aware of the fiscal constraints of nonprofit organizations. Often, people who manage projects within the nonprofit structure are passionate about mission realization with a nearly complete disregard for cost efficiency or cost effectiveness. Every program or service that appears to serve the targeted community appears necessary. By putting fiscal responsibility in the hands of project managers and by evaluating project managers on their ability to control costs, more rational expense decisions will likely be made. The weakness of this approach is that project managers could focus too much on the bottom line and become "overly corporate," thereby neglecting our constituents. One way to overcome this threat is to include randomly selected consumer evaluations as a component of employee performance appraisals, which makes sense because high-quality customer service is another—and long overdue—trend in our industry.

Our department is presented with the following opportunities in support of the implementation of the proposed departmental redesign plan. First, motivation is present throughout SDSA for the change, which was initiated by the board of trustees earlier this year. Second, funding for our department is currently limited. Therefore, rotating projects among our staff allows current employees to cover program areas that are not addressed under the current organizational design. Third, our department staff works well together. Implementing a more complicated organizational design that continues to layer staff members above and below one another could likely disrupt this harmony. Fourth, people are looking to the new department director for new ideas and leadership, which means that new strategies will be given more objective evaluation than approaches proposed by organizational leaders with a history at SDSA. Finally, implementation of the proposed departmental redesign is supported by the current average age of our staff—approximately 24 years old. These young professionals realize that they need to gain much more experience in all of the areas within our department if they plan to advance their careers in the nonprofit sector. Furthermore, the staff has indicated a willingness to learn.

Nonetheless, some constraints exist to implementing the proposed organizational redesign. First, the human resources department may have a problem with the generalist hiring approach suggested by the proposal. They may argue the necessity of providing new hires with specific job responsibilities so that performance evaluation criteria can be made clear to them. Obviously, the proposed redesign makes this task a little more difficult. Second, because this new structure is innovative, finding professionals who want to be a part of this change may be an obstacle. Third, the increased training associated with the proposed redesign will require a financial investment that other leaders in the organization may not support. Fourth, in the short term, project expenses will increase because rotated project managers will not have a history in managing certain programs and services. Finally, and perhaps most controversial, our constituents will not know who to identify with specific programs and services. The proposed redesign forces interested constituents to form relationships with our entire department staff rather than one or two individuals, regardless of the way they have interacted with the organization in the past.

The restructuring of our department is necessary to ensure our future vitality. Specifically, we must find new ways to maintain our connection with the public and the rest of the organization. The need for creativity and innovation within our department is necessary if we desire to continue to deliver the programs and services we currently provide to our constituents. New ideas and strategies are imperative. The proposed departmental redesign is just one step toward more efficient and effective operations within our department.

Thank you for your time.

Sarah N.: Thank you, Deborah. We are open for comments.

Ann S.: I am impressed with the Arthritis Foundation, which has developed a disease management program (self-help courses, exercise programs, aquatic program) that will improve knowledge; increase self-care; reduce pain, physician visits, and depression; and increase self-esteem and functional ability. This packaged course has been shown to save health plans $425,000 per 100,000 covered lives over four years. They are funded by several HMOs to run these courses. Can we do something like this?

Deborah L.: We don't have anyone on the staff of our society who could develop this.

Ann S.: Whether we should develop such programs depends, in part, on what we are all about as a society.

Sarah N.: What advice should we give Deborah so she can revise this plan before it goes to our full board meeting in two weeks?

Ann S.: How will you know if you are successful in terms of outcomes? For example, on the web site, are you recording the number of "connects" or "hits"? Do you have a counter for which sections of our web site are being visited?

John S.: Other web sites, like the American Cancer Society's, have found that many people connect with their web site after they or a close friend or relative have just been diagnosed with cancer and they are really ready to learn at this time. If our web site focuses on fund raising, will this drive away the people who need us for education and help?

Deborah L.: Original content like this is not easy to develop and will take time.

Steven K.: Healthcare is changing, as we all know. Cost control, managed care, disease management, capitation, outcomes, measurement, and clinical guidelines are all affecting our patients whose care can be expensive. Because our people need costly care, HMOs are not out to attract them. Can we use our advocacy system to help with this problem?

Short Case F | Charity Health System

Charity Health System (CHS)—comprised of four owned and two managed hospitals, multiple ambulatory care sites, a freestanding same-day surgery facility, a home health agency, and multiple physician practices owned by the system network and a very successful joint venture HMO product—operates in the mid-Atlantic region, perhaps the most competitive healthcare environment in the country.

The system has made significant strides in operating and managing clinical and support departments across its acute and ambulatory components. The medical staff are credentialed across the system and in the system-based medical departments such as pathology, anesthesia, and radiology; the physicians are members of single groups in which the president of the group holds an exclusive contract for that discipline's services across the system and, in turn, employs the member physicians.

At the request of the health system, the radiology group, Charity Imaging Services, went through a reorganization prior to developing a systemwide contract. The group transitioned from a model of equal partnership with a rotating president slot to a model whereby one partner, the group president, holds a majority vote, full accountability and authority for delivering a quality service systemwide, and is the named holder of the exclusivity contract.

The reorganization sparked some internal conflicts for the group and nine members (of 14) decided to leave. Among those leaving was a radiologist who had earned a significant reputation in the surrounding area medical community as an innovative and very skilled interventionalist. He was immediately hired by a local competitor.

All nine physicians were immediately replaced. Two interventional radiologists with excellent credentials were part of the replacement staff recruited by the group president who also happened to be an interventionalist.

At the end of the first 12 months, it was apparent that the new IR staff members were not working out for both performance and interpersonal relationship reasons. Within the broader radiology physician community, Charity Imaging Services group problems were known, as well as the medical staff's displeasure with the level of service, particularly within the interventional section.

The system's executive staff were increasingly concerned as the radiology volume numbers began to indicate a steady decline in interventional procedures and consequently related vascular volume, an area in which they had always had a very strong market share. They also feared a halo effect on all other radiology services.

In addition to the major clinical service issues, the group president, while enjoying an excellent clinical reputation, was judged by many not to be an effective department leader. She became bogged down in operational issues that should have been handled by the department managers, whom she consistently micromanaged. In the meantime, the major issues of physician performance, recruitment and development, and maintaining relationships with the attending referring staff did not receive the attention they warranted.

A New Opportunity

In the physician community over the last several years, discussion levels have risen around the converging skills of interventional radiologists, vascular surgeons, and cardiologists as arterial stenting and other advanced vascular technologies continue to emerge and significantly alter the established approaches to treating vascular disease. The three physician groups, in addition to providing state-of-the-art quality care, are also rightly concerned about protecting a referral base, especially as the large baby boomer generation ages and begins to experience peripheral vascular diseases.

Aware of the situation at CHS, several well-trained and very reputable interventional radiologists approached the health system executives and proposed the development of a multidisciplinary vascular center. Within the CHS, they were aware that the predominant cardiology group, known for their clinical excellence and service orientation, were interested in the concept, as was the main vascular surgery group associated with the system. The vascular surgery group had in fact just recruited a new surgeon who had recently completed a combined vascular surgery/interventional radiology fellowship. The landscape was changing quickly and it was the belief of these IRs that an opportunity existed to be in the forefront of implementing emerging technologies in a multidisciplinary program that would achieve market prominence through clinical service excellence. In exchange for spearheading this collaborative initiative, they sought the exclusive contract for interventional and vascular lab diagnostic services across the system. They proposed to pay a "tax" to the radiology group for the exclusivity and believed that, through the development of a clinically excellent program, the radiologist would perform more diagnostic work as more patients flowed through the system. In addition to the economic potential this presented for the radiologists, a vascular institute presented an economic opportunity for all services, as well as the health system, to increase volume. In addition, all would benefit from recognition as a center of vascular excellence.

Case Question

1. How should management at Charity Health System respond to this situation?

Part IV

Professional Integration

Introduction

The power of physicians and nurses has changed over the decades of this century, and not in unison. Before the Flexner reforms of 1910 (which called for a reduction in the number of medical schools in the United States and established stringent criteria for medical training), a few months of education would qualify one to become a physician, producing lots of lower-income physicians. A wealthy patient could and did pay for a full-time physician or private duty nurse. As medical schools were closed following the Flexner reforms, reduction in the number of practitioners occurred slowly. Many physicians struggled during the Depression, as did hospital administrators who took large pay cuts to hold their jobs. The growth of health insurance after World War II led to a so-called golden era of medicine as cost-based reimbursement of Medicare and Blue Cross supported the growth of hospitals and their staff, and nursing education largely moved out of the hospital and into the college and university.

In the postwar era, physicians held—and wielded—great power. The most likely reason a hospital administrator would lose his job was because the medical staff wanted to get rid of him. Physicians, not pleased with a hospital, could easily shift their admissions to another nearby facility. Increasingly, hospitals added new equipment and services to attract specialists. Reaction to the rising costs that resulted included prospective payment (DRGs), capitation (HMOs, PPOs) and price competition among managed care plans. The health plans discovered how to provide care with fewer hospitals, fewer hospital beds, and fewer support and clinical staff. Downsizing in hospitals in the late 1990s became routine, leaving more nurses than available positions in some locations. Specialists, in particular, have experienced the effects of competitive managed care on the need for physicians. What will be the steady state for physician supply and demand? A diversion into labor economics is needed to predict this future. Most physicians and nurses will not earn the incomes of some professional athletes whose presence at a game can sell more tickets, popcorn, and souvenirs. The pay of stars, including physician stars, can be linked to their drawing power. The other extreme is the fast food restaurant, like McDonald's, which provides the same hamburger in 80 or more countries largely using minimum-wage part-time labor. McDonald's management has done this by designing a working environment that makes it nearly impossible to make a bad batch of french fries.

Nursing and medicine will fall within these extremes of income and power. A good physician, nurse, or primary care practice can draw patients like a magnet. If this group can attract 3,000 new subscribers to an HMO at $150 per member per month (3,000 × $150 × 12) that creates a gross income for their HMO of $5.4 million. Care teams that patients brag about are economically valuable to the HMO. Conversely, specialists may only cost money rather than attract new enrollees. The result is a shift in the balance of power between primary and specialty care. The successful managed care plan wants to attract these "platinum" primary care provider groups. It wants to educate them to improve their practice and it wants to retain them.

The two case studies in this section exemplify new approaches to reorganizing clinical practice, which is increasingly clinician-led. The "Physician Leadership: MetroHealth System of Cleveland" case describes the overhaul in management/medical staff relations brought about by a new leadership. Of note is the successful effort of this leadership to compete in the Cleveland market as a public hospital. The "Primary Care Instrument Panel" case shows the process a managed care plan uses to transform the way performance is considered and rewarded.

Today, the medical profession retains its basic and legally enforced monopoly over the key functions of healthcare, as physicians are the sole authority in diagnosing and carrying out the treatment of health problems. The basis of their decision making has been experience and clinical judgment. Increasingly, this informal, unchallengeable mode of decision making is being replaced under physician supervision, by "evidence-based" medicine, which requires evidence of effectiveness, population-based reasoning, clinical decision analysis, cost-effectiveness analysis, utilization review, clinical paths, guidelines or algorithms, process improvement thinking, outcomes, health status and quality of life measurements, and comparative cost analysis.

Physicians can rely on numerous sources of power in dealing with managers, including the protection afforded them by organizations and medical staff bylaws or through negotiated contracts. They may use the authority based on their knowledge of medicine to demand resources from the managers such as additional staff, space, and equipment. Physicians are often respected by nurses and other employees. They may have access to board members and community leaders who are their patients. Their power may stem from the ability to enlist the support of other physicians as a group or from their lack of dependence on a specific institution for referral of patients.

Physicians expect recognition, acceptance, and trust from the manager, and they expect that their livelihood will not be threatened by managerial initiative. Physicians are concerned about their status and power compared to other occupational groups, to other physicians within the organization, and to physicians working at competing institutions. They want to determine their own working conditions and to be provided with support services adequate to house, feed, and care for their patients. Physicians do not like to waste time in endless or frequent meetings, and they expect to be consulted if organizational policy changes will affect them.

These seem like reasonable expectations. Why, then, does the physician feel that expectations are not met by the organization and its managers? Other physicians may be competing for limited resources of funds, space, and staff; demand may change for one specialty compared to others. The manager may have a different concept of time wasting: completing records represents time not reimbursed to the physician, but a necessary cash flow to the HCO. Sometimes events move too quickly for adequate consultation, or medical staff officials and staff physicians do not communicate with each other.

For example, a manager may ask the chief of staff, a department head, or the medical board for approval of implementation of a risk-management program, provision of financial guarantees to recruit family practitioners, or appointment of a new chief of emergency medicine. Medical officials may give informal approval and get back to physicians in each department for further discussion and recommendations for action. In the interim, however, time, money, and skilled personnel may no longer be available to the same extent. Even after policies are agreed upon, the manager often finds the physicians have misinterpreted what medical officials agreed to at staff meetings or misread committee minutes. Following implementation of new policies, physicians may personally object and subsequently practice a poor quality of medicine. Yet they may fail to understand why their peers do not honor what seems to them to be legitimate requests. Further, a physician's interests may conflict with organizational goals.

Similarly, the manager expects recognition, acceptance, and trust from the physician. She expects physicians to be concerned about organizational goals such as cost containment and quality improvement. The manager expects the physician to fulfill specific organizational commitments agreed to in advance, such as punctual attendance at meetings of the medical committee that the physician chairs. The manager does not expect to be attacked personally when she and a physician disagree on an issue. She expects respect for her organizational role and responsibility for internal coordination of activities and adaptation of the organization to external pressures. The manager expects the physician not to waste her time but, for example, to try to solve a problem first with the involved department head whose lack of timely response to the physician's request may, after all, be reasonable. The manager expects to be consulted if an action by a medical official or attending physician will affect the organization's goal attainment or system maintenance.

These expectations seem reasonable as well. Why, then, don't physicians meet them? Physicians may not view the manager as she views herself; they may view her as a supporter of clinical services rather than as an organizational coordinator or integrator. They may see the manager as working *for* them rather than *with* them to attain organizational goals. Many physicians may fear the manager because of increasing dependence on the organization for their livelihood. Managers, through their influence on budget determination and their control of information, may affect the physician's access to scarce resources.

If physicians can discredit the manager, the manager will have less power over them. Physicians are accustomed to giving orders, not to taking them. If the manager is actively attempting to increase revenues and decrease expenses, physicians can surely find fault. (The manager did not consult sufficiently with them, she did not consult sufficiently in advance, or she has favored certain other departments in budget and staff.) Further, physicians may object to the manager's tone, style, travel schedule, number of assistants, size of office, or salary.

Physicians will often disagree with the manager over policy. For example, physicians at Alpha Hospital may decide that expensive equipment will help in their daily practice, and surgeons at neighboring Beta Hospital are getting more sophisticated equipment. Alpha Hospital's policy of providing services to the chronically ill will therefore not help surgeons stay competitive or increase their incomes. Or physicians may have a conflict of interest with the hospital; given a certain amount of capitation income, for instance, more money for the physicians means less for the hospital, and vice versa.

Most physician behavior has no effective organizational responsibility system. Physicians can take "cheap shots" at the manager if they are not effectively accountable to anyone in the organizational structure for incurring costs or ensuring quality and access. Non-paid physician department chiefs and committee chairs are usually more interested in maintaining their physician networks of patient referral than in attaining organizational goals. Physicians work long hours and they consider the competing and conflicting demands on their time more important than certain organizational obligations, even those to which they have agreed in advance.

Finally, physicians may distrust the manager, find the manager incompetent, or dislike the manager personally. This may be because of the manager's actions or inaction, ranging from gaining board approval for a CT scanner to responding appropriately to low nursing morale. Increasingly physicians are being hired by HCOs, in part, because they are more likely to be obeyed than non-physician managers. Many physician managers quickly learn, however, that, to the extent they are paid by the organization and no longer practice medicine, are increasingly viewed as "one of them" rather than as "one of us" by many practicing physicians.

Given the inherent difficulties, what opportunities do managers have to perform effectively and yet maintain decent working relationships with physicians and other clinicians? Is this even possible? Managers can exchange scarce resources of money, staff and space with clinicians in return for assistance in goal attainment. Managers can order clinicians to implement decisions, calculating that clinicians lack the power to resist effectively. Managers can persuade clinicians to act in the long-term interest of the organization, the patient, and the consumer. The manager has a limited amount of political "chips" to spend, just as she has a limited amount of organizational funds available. The manager can invest in political power by building good informal relationships with key clinicians, or she can spend power in making decisions opposed by key clinicians or groups. Timing, tone, body language, and judgment are all important for the manager whose tenure may well vary conversely with activism.

The manager has resources available that the clinician lacks. She may have influence with the governing board regarding long-range planning decisions, influence on appointment of physicians and nurses to paid and unpaid positions, access to grants and gifts, and influence on rates of clinician remuneration. The manager may have special knowledge useful in advising clinicians on business and personal problems and to do personal favors for them, or have information concerning results of implementing proposed strategic initiatives at other HCOs.

Even as the physician has medical authority for patient care decisions, the manager has authority based on expertise in marketing and government regulation. Often competitive and regulatory requirements can be interpreted by managers to rationalize decisions that will benefit patients and consumers at the expense or inconvenience of clinicians. The manager may also accrue a certain authority because of long tenure in a position, having gained the trust of clinicians with similar tenure. When a manager has gained such trust, others will back critical decisions or disagree in private or in advance, without personal attacks.

The manager can persuade clinicians of the justice or advantage of policy or administrative decisions. Of course, some clinicians will not wish to be persuaded. It is not difficult to wake up someone who is asleep—but it is hard to wake someone who is pretending to be asleep.

The manager can help clinicians obtain the resources they need, which may be in the organization's interest as well. The manager may delay implementation of what clinicians oppose until a more favorable time. Above all, the manager must know what she is doing, be sure of her facts, and be conservative in her forecasts. As in other fields, nothing succeeds like success or fails like failure, and often the failing manager will not be given a second chance.

The two cases "Physician Leadership" and "Primary Care Instrument Panel" approach similar organizational problems of remaining competitive by improving quality, making services more customer-focused, and containing costs. Both cases focus on physician leadership to bring along the physicians, sooner rather than later.

Case Questions

Physician Leadership: MetroHealth System of Cleveland

1. What are the most important factors at MetroHealth that affect physician-management relations?
2. What are some of the ways in which integration of physicians relative to the goals of a hospital system can be effectively measured?
3. To what extent does the payment system at Metro influence physician performance?
4. In what ways is Dr. Estes a successful physician leader?
5. To what extent is physician commitment to organizational mission and strategy key to Metro's relative success in the market place? How appropriate is the extent of physician leadership?
6. To what extent is physician commitment to organizational mission and strategy key to MetroHealth's relative success in the *medical* market place?

The Primary Care Instrument Panel

1. Design the physician "instrument panel." What should be in it?
2. Justify your rationale for these components. How costly would it be to obtain this information?
3. What is needed to implement your goal of an appropriate instrument panel? (Just defining the ideal does not get you there.)
4. Compare the spider diagram and control chart approaches. Which would you recommend and why?
5. Design a "just-in-time" education program to respond to requests from physician groups. What topics should be covered?
6. For a high-priority topic, outline the content of the educational module.

Selected Bibliography

Accreditation Manual for Hospitals, 1999 Edition. Chicago: Joint Commission on Accreditation of Health Care Organizations, 1998.

Brecher C. (ed.) *Managing Safety-Net Hospitals*, Chicago: Health Administration Press, 1993.

Eisenberg, J. *Doctors' Decisions and the Cost of Medical Care*, Chicago: Health Administration Press, 1986.

Fishman, L. E., "What Types of Hospitals Form the Safety Net?" *Health Affairs* 16, no. 4 (July–Aug 1997): 215–22.

Griffith, J. R., *Designing 21st Century Healthcare*, Chicago: Health Administration Press, 1998.

Griffith J. R., "Measuring Performance" in J. R. Griffith, *The Well-Managed Healthcare Organization,* 4th Edition, Chicago: Health Administration Press, 1999, pp. 185–242.

Kindig, D. A., *Purchasing Population Health*, Ann Arbor, MI: University of Michigan Press, 1997.

LeTourneau, B. and W. Curry, "Physicians as Executives: Boon or Boondoggle?" *Frontiers of Health Services Management* 13, no. 3, (Spring 1997): 3–25.

Pyenson, B. S., *Managing Risk,* Chicago: AHA Publishing Company, 1998.

Zelman, W. A. and R. A. Berenson, *The Managed Care Blues and How to Cure Them,* Washington, DC: Georgetown University Press, 1998.

Case 9 | The Physician-Led Organization

Anthony R. Kovner

As of fall 1998, key changes shaping the Cleveland health system included the following: increasing concentration in the hospital market, expansion of high-end medical services, health plans facing stiff price competition and internal administrative difficulties, and employers not pursuing aggressive purchasing strategies.[1] Three local institutions—the Cleveland Clinic, University Hospitals Health System (UH), and the former Blues plan, Medical Mutual of Ohio—retain dominance in the market.

Market Description

The Cleveland Clinic owns 40 percent of the hospital beds in Cuyahoga County (population 2.2 million) and 30 percent in the broader six-county primary metropolitan statistical area, compared with UH's 11 percent. (See Illustration 9.1 for Cuyahoga County hospitals.) While the two local not-for-profit hospital systems have grown, the two for-profit systems have lost market share over the last two years. MetroHealth, the county's public hospital, continues to be the leading provider of charity care and Medicaid services. (For Metro service locations, see Illustration 9.2.) Metro retains a close relationship with the Cleveland Clinic, participating as a lead member of the Cleveland Health Network (CHN).

Cleveland has been viewed as a specialty-oriented healthcare market with considerable excess hospital capacity. The expiration of Ohio's certificate-of-need has resulted in new construction and technology investments by hospitals. Clear competition also exists among health plans. Premium levels have been flat or have declined during the past year. Most plans share the same broad provider networks. Purchasers

ILLUSTRATION 9.1
Cuyahoga County Hospitals

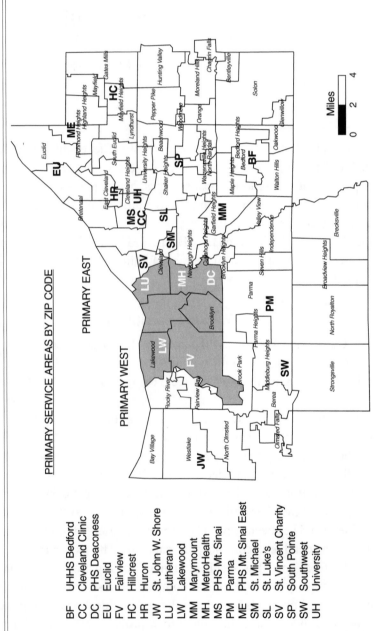

PRIMARY SERVICE AREAS BY ZIP CODE

BF   UHHS Bedford
CC   Cleveland Clinic
DC   PHS Deaconess
EU   Euclid
FV   Fairview
HC   Hillcrest
HR   Huron
JW   St. John W. Shore
LU   Lutheran
LW   Lakewood
MM   Marymount
MH   MetroHealth
MS   PHS Mt. Sinai
PM   Parma
ME   PHS Mt. Sinai East
SM   St. Michael
SL   St. Luke's
SV   St. Vincent Charity
SP   South Pointe
SW   Southwest
UH   University

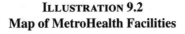

ILLUSTRATION 9.2
Map of MetroHealth Facilities

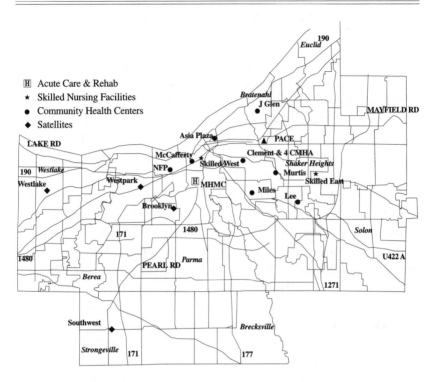

(employers)have not increased their demands for highly managed care insurance products nor turned to direct contracting to get more control over costs and quality.

Medicaid plans are having financial difficulties. The state's payment rates have declined and competition among the plans has increased. The number of Medicaid plans is expected to decline further as the state implements enrollment floors in each county, under which only plans that enroll 10 percent or more of the eligible population will be allowed to contract with Medicaid. MetroHealth is Ohio's largest provider of Medicaid services.

Overview of the MetroHealth System

The mission statement of the MetroHealth System is as follows:

The MetroHealth System commits to leadership in providing healthcare services that continually improve the health of the people in our community. We offer an integrated program of services provided through a system that encompasses a partnership between management and physicians and reflects excellence in patient care supported by superior education and research programs. We are committed to responding to community needs, improving the health status of our region, and controlling healthcare costs.

Metro is licensed to operate 680 beds, of which 524 are staffed and in use. Metro also operates two skilled nursing centers with an additional 490+ beds, a network of 16 ambulatory care centers offering primary care services in various locations, and three substance abuse treatment centers. The medical center's 41-acre campus is located on the near west side of the city of Cleveland, approximately two miles from downtown. All facilities are fully accredited.

Since 1914, Metro has been a major teaching affiliate of Case Western Reserve University and provides 40 to 50 percent of all clinical hours for university medical students. Grant funding for Metro's Center for Research and Education from the National Institutes of Health was more than $10.8 million in 1997, as compared with $3.8 million in 1992.

Cuyahoga County provides financial support for Metro through annual appropriations from a portion of the proceeds of two voted property tax levies for health and human services and, from time to time, its general fund. Metro trustees are appointed jointly by the Board of County Commissioners and the senior judges of the probate and common pleas courts. They serve without compensation for six-year overlapping terms and may be reappointed upon the expiration of their terms. By law, the composition of the trustees must be bipartisan with equal representation from the two major political parties.

Metro houses a Level I trauma center (highest level of complexity), serving as the regional burn center for northeast Ohio and northwest Pennsylvania. The Neonatal Intensive Care Unit is one of three Level III (highest level of complexity) nurseries in Cleveland. The Center for Rehabilitation is a distinct 143-bed acute rehabilitation center and one of the largest in the country. Metro operates Metro Life Flight, the nation's second busiest aeromedical transport service, with four owned helicopters.

Two-thirds of Metro's 21,536 discharged patients (excluding normal newborns) live in its primary service area, whose population is approximately 500,000. In 1996, Metro accounted for 9.18 percent of the 193,802 county patients (excluding normal newborns) discharged from Ohio hospitals. In the primary service area, which alone accounted for 46.4 percent of all discharges in the county, Metro captured the largest share of the market at 16.7 percent. Metro was a market leader in burns (70.7 percent), rehabilitation (58.3 percent), neonatology (19.2 percent) and obstetrics (18.5 percent). Metro provided more than 500,000 outpatient visits in 1997 (see Illustration 9.3 for Metro utilization statistics).

Metro's medical staff is organized into 16 major departments, each with a full-time chair. There are more than 350 employed physicians in each of these departments as of 1998, as shown in Illustration 9.4, and more than 300 residents. Total medical staff includes 238 associate staff, 193 adjunct or affiliate staff, plus 71 bioscientific, emeritus, or honorary staff members. Metro employs 5,562 full- and part-time employees, including the active medical staff. Approximately 2,000 of these employees are union members.

RELATIONSHIP BETWEEN MANAGEMENT AND THE MEDICAL STAFF

Metro's CEO, Terry White, has previous leadership experience at Lutheran Hospital, University Hospital of Cleveland, and University Hospital of Cincinnati. He has been MetroHealth CEO for five years. According to Mr. White, organizations are made up of people, structure, and process. In 1994, the hospital lacked such proper structure and process. Since then, Mr. White has been developing a grand alliance with the medical staff to have one rather than two management groups. He has tried, in his direction of the institution, to create a culture incorporating physician leaders. Going beyond the tokenism of board representation or the installation of a medical director, he has tried to build a physician-driven organization, with medical leadership and accountability.

When Mr. White started at Metro, a high-quality medical staff was in place, functioning under an employment model. This model had 17 different medical departments, with separate practice plans, and no oversight and accountability. Chairs were responsible for more than $100 million dollars of budget, half of which came from practice revenue and half from hospital subsidy. The senior medical officer position was short-tenured and the occupants were neither respected nor empowered. The credentials of chief medical officers were mediocre in research and in

ILLUSTRATION 9.3
MetroHealth Medical Center Utilization Statistics, 1995–97

Indicator	1995	1996	1997
Staffed Beds	532	532	524
Occupancy Rate*	65.5	58.6	56.9
Occupancy Rate**	64.8	58.4	57.2
Licensed Beds	728	728	728
Occupancy Rate	47.9	42.9	41.0
Discharges	21,603	19,913	18,036
Patient Days	127,180	113,868	108,863
ALOS (no newborns)	5.9	5.7	6.0
Newborn Bassinets	48	48	48
Number of Births	3,823	3,910	3,719
Newborn Days	10,010	9,755	10,531
ALOS (including newborns)	5.4	5.2	5.5

*Excludes newborns
**Includes newborns
Notes: Effective May 13, 1996, 29 Rehabilitation beds were changed to Skilled Nursing beds.
1. Staffed Beds, 1995–1997 all exclude Nursery bassinets. However, 1996 and 1997 include 29 Subacute beds.
2. Licensed beds include 48 Nursery bassinets and the 29 Subacute beds. (In 1995 the 29 beds were Rehabilitation).
3. The discharges and patient days for 1996 and 1997 *exclude* both newborn and subacute activities.

business. No one wanted a really strong person to occupy this post. Under the previous CEO, the chairs had direct access to the CEO for most key management decisions.

In 1995, the interim chief of staff retired, and Mr. White hired a national search firm to recruit a successor. The search committee, led by a physician who was not a department chair, was composed of "physicians of the future," rather than being chair-dominated. Dr. Melinda Estes, who was finally selected as chief of staff, had unassailable credentials, including an MBA, a great number of publications, impeccable training as a neuropathologist, and her own research lab; in addition, she was the first woman on the board of governors at the Cleveland Clinic, where she was also associate chief of staff. Dr. Estes was also articulate, with good interpersonal skills.

Mr. White wants Metro to be a physician-led organization; therefore, he sees his job as empowering the chief of staff to do this. She is in charge of the medical staff, and the department chairs, who are not allowed to make end runs to the CEO, report to her. In addition, MetroHealth

ILLUSTRATION 9.4
Number of Physicians by Major Medical
Departments (as of July 22, 1998)

Department	Active Staff
Anesthesiology	18
Dentistry	7
Dermatology	4
Emergency Medicine	19
Family Practice	27
Medicine	95
Neurology	2
Ob/Gyn	21
Orthopaedics	14
Otolaryngology	2
Pathology	9
Pediatrics	52
P M & R	18
Psychiatry	21
Radiology	24
Surgery	31
Total	364

Management Council (MMC) was created. Before any major recommendation goes to the governing board, it must be agreed to and processed by the MMC. (See Appendix 9.1 for the MMC management protocol.)

What Mr. White has asked of physicians in return is accountability—that they support the institutional mission and be accountable for it. For the first time, the budget for 1999 integrated medical and hospital revenues by service. Results for physicians are measured in terms of productivity rather than revenues—otherwise, practice plans could be successful but slip into providing a lower standard of care for non-paying patients.

Mr. White sees his main functions as CEO as helping develop Metro's vision and strategy, managing the board relationship, supporting the organization and fundraising, and building a structure to accomplish the Metro mission. He carries out his duties as CEO through a goals and objectives process.

Participation in Managed Care

Metro has approximately 35,000 covered lives in managed care, approximately two-thirds of whom are women and children covered by Ohio's mandatory Medicaid program. More than 12,000 covered managed care lives are not on Medicaid. Metro employees have a fee-for-service insurance program, and managed-care contracts with all the major insurance companies. Metro is part of the CHN network for managed-care contracts, which was set up with the Cleveland Clinic. Being part of a network has also enabled economies in purchasing, as Metro is able to access Premier, a multi-hospital organization, which negotiates national contracts with suppliers for a broad range of products. Collaboration with other providers has also involved clinical services. For example, Metro was losing $1.7 million annually on renal inpatient services until it formed a joint venture with another provider of renal services. The partnership has resulted in a $400,000 annual surplus that enables Metro resources to capitalize satellite centers, which results in more people served in a more cost-effective way. By gaining control of these costs, Metro's 1998 costs were below those in 1994.

Metro is the largest Medicaid provider in Ohio, both in terms of fee-for-service and managed care. Managed-care revenue makes up less than 20 percent of total Metro revenue. (Metro still has a large fee-for-service Medicaid business because of turnover of beneficiaries who lose eligibility in the Medicaid program and because the disabled are not yet included in the mandatory program.) A number of competitors in this market have either pulled out or gone bankrupt, and only four HMOs in Cuyahoga County cover Medicaid managed care beneficiaries.

Metro receives full-risk capitation under its Medicaid HMO contracts. HMOs administer payment for services rendered by other providers to Metro Health Services members. This typically accounts for 15 to 20 percent of the premium and is applied against MHS gross capitation. Metro receives the net premium less HMO management fees (which average 15 percent). The state and county have retained vendors to manage enrollment. Metro is losing money on Medicaid managed care because of a variety of factors, including utilization, inadequate premium, and high HMO administrative costs. Although Metro is losing 10 to 15 percent on every contract, providing services to these beneficiaries is part of Metro's public mission; therefore it must continue these contracts.

Metro's managed care panel includes 107 primary care practitioners and 366 specialists. Before contracts are negotiated they are reviewed by the MMC. Metro issues quarterly statements and reports on inpatient utilization, showing where they are losing money. Metro views the Medicaid managed care capitation rate set by the state as too low. In addition, the utilization targets that form the actuarial premises for these premiums are not realistic, given the population served. Metro's Utilization Committee now has data on a per-doctor level which may, in the future, be related to physician compensation.

Development of Ambulatory Care Networks

Eight of Metro's satellites are in the city and four are in the suburbs, in addition to ambulatory care provided at the main hospital site. These satellites were developed to expand access and support managed care penetration for all payers. Set up to work like private practice models, the suburban satellites grew 20 percent in 1998. Patients are attracted to their own physicians, who are employed by Metro, and who often have roots in the community. The suburban satellites break even and the urban centers lose money.

Physicians under managed care are under pressure to be more productive. Base salary is now structured so that part is variable based on relative value units delivered. The physician leadership in ambulatory care is integrated within the system leadership structure, sits on all committees, and is involved in future planning. The medical operations unit provides support to the physician leadership in ambulatory satellites. Ambulatory care is a competitive market, with other hospital systems locating new sites to funnel off paying business from the Metro satellites.

Regarding ambulatory care strategy, Dr. Harry Walker, the medical director for the Center for Community Health, put it this way: "It's hard to be successful if you lock yourself into being only a public hospital. We can't lose the mission, but economic realities have to be co-equal. We must be efficient even where we are losing money, so as to use precious resources to the best advantage." Dr. Walker finds physicians more committed now to the defined strategic goals of the organization. "There is a challenge in staying alive in a competitive market, facing up to reality, but physician leaders have been brought in who want the system to work. There is a higher trust level now, more of a shared responsibility; before, there were two separate decision making groups—medical and administrative."

Keeping Financially Healthy

Metro financials are healthy (see Illustration 9.5 for 1995–1997 comparative data) and have improved since 1995. Comparing 1997 to 1995, occupancy is down 13 percent (to 57 percent), discharges are down 16.5 percent, and inpatient days are down 14.4 percent. However, total outpatient visits are up 12 percent, and gross revenues are up 1.7 percent. This total includes a 21 percent increase in commercial insurance revenues. Net revenues are down 0.25 percent. Total gross revenues were $341 million and charity and bad debt costs were almost $44 million, a 13.6 percent decrease from 1995. Metro received a $17.8 million governmental subsidy in 1997. This subsidy will be $24 million for 1999.

Healthcare is a large part of the Cleveland economy. According to surveys, Metro has a positive image with the public, and residency programs have a good image with those seeking residencies, as reflected in the match results. Although many people in the greater Cleveland area may not know that Metro is a public hospital, MetroHealth lags in awareness by the public and favorableness relative to its primary competitors. The system approach with satellites has improved its image. Metro's primary care community is mainly the working poor, rather than the unemployed. And it is not located in an area with many competing hospitals of comparable clinical stature and capability.

Several of the current top Metro managers came from the Cleveland Clinic. Physicians working at Metro are proud of their mission and excited by taking cases that others don't want. But Metro cannot just rely on government status and subsidies, and physicians understand this— 1999 was the first year in which medical and administrative budgets were integrated. Department chiefs became accountable, fiscally, for their whole product line.

One result of the integration was to change physicians' schedules to enhance productivity. For example, in surgery, schedules were changed from whatever surgeons wanted to what maximizes revenue utilization and level scheduling. Prior to the schedule changes, a surgeon had a clinic schedule every day, that was never filled, and all the patients were directed to show at 1:00 p.m. Now the surgeon is scheduled for one or two afternoons and the schedule is full.

ILLUSTRATION 9.5
MetroHealth Medical Center Comparative Data 1995–1997

	1995	1997	% Change		
Number of Staffed Beds	532	524	–1.50%		
Number of Births	3823	3595	–5.96%		
Occupancy Rate	65.50%	56.92%	–13.10%		
*Discharges**	*1995*	*1995%*	*1997*	*1997%*	*% Change*
Medicare	5,372	24.87%	4,330	24.01%	–19.40%
Medicaid	8,753	40.52%	7,177	39.79%	–18.01%
Commercial Insurance	4,672	21.63%	4,560	25.28%	–2.40%
Self-Pay	2,806	12.99%	1,969	10.92%	–29.83%
Other					
Total Discharges	21,603	100.00%	18,036	100.00%	–16.51%
Inpatient Days	*1995*	*1995%*	*1997*	*1997%*	*% Change*
Medicare	41,175	32.38%	31,758	29.17%	–22.87%
Medicaid	46,611	36.65%	38,392	35.27%	–17.63%
Commercial Insurance	29.699	23.35%	30,556	28.07%	2.89%
Self-Pay	9,695	7.62%	8,157	7.49%	–15.86%
Other					
Total Inpatient Days	127,180	100.00%	108,863	100.00%	–14.40%
	1995	*1997*	*% Change*		
Total Emergency Department	58,176	51,445	–11.57%		
Total Outpatient Department Visits	560,670	628,328	12.07%		
Total Outpatient Visits	*1995*	*1995%*	*1997*	*1997%*	*% Change*
Medicare	79,110	14.11%	96,386	15.34%	21.84%
Medicaid	196,235	35.00%	223,371	35.55%	13.83%
Commercial Insurance	141,233	25.19%	177,691	28.28%	25.81%
Self-Pay	144,092	25.70%	130,880	20.83%	–9.17%
Other					
Total Outpatient Visits	560.670	100.00%	628,328	100.00%	12.07%
Gross Revenues (in thousands)	*1995*	*1995%*	*1997*	*1997%*	*% Change*
Medicare	$82,651	24.64%	$79,707	23.35%	–3.56%
Medicaid	$118,588	35.35%	$109,519	32.09%	–7.65%
Commercial Insurance	$85,499	25.48%	$103,550	30.34%	21.11%
Self-Pay	$48,750	14.53%	$48,527	14.22%	–0.46%
Other					
Total Gross Revenues	$335,488	100.00%	$341,303	100.00%	1.73%
Net Revenues (in thousands)	*1995*	*1995%*	*1997*	*1997%*	*% Change*
Medicare	$74,421	28.07%	$71,786	27.14%	–3.54%
Medicaid	$85,163	32.12%	$72,967	27.59%	–14.32%
Commercial Insurance	$61,504	23.20%	$67,495	25.52%	9.74%
Self-Pay	$2,115	0.80%	$2,570	0.97%	21.51%
Medicaid DSH	$30,905	11.66%	$31,852	12.04%	3.06%
Local Gov. Appropriation	$11,012	4.15%	$17,800	6.73%	61.64%
Total Net Revenues	$265,120	100.00%	$264,470	100.00%	–0.25%
Uncompensated Care Costs	*1995*	*1995%*	*1997*	*1997%*	*% Change*
(in thousands)		*of Costs*		*of Costs*	
Charity Care & Bad Debt Costs	$50,846	16.33%	$43,918	14.68%	–13.63%

*This data does not include subacute discharges or newborn days and discharges.
Source: NAPH Survey for both years. Only reflects the Medical Center activities.

For medical operations support, departments are organized into a small number of clusters. One such cluster is surgery, ENT, orthopaedics, anesthesia, cardiology, and pulmonary. The operations manager is taking scheduling away from medical secretaries into a central scheduling system. Waiting lists are being reduced. Because of better scheduling, for example, the wait for eye exams has been reduced to 3–4 weeks from 6–8. Physicians stay later, allowing for three additional appointments per physician each afternoon. Metro collects only 30 percent of billings from the surgical cluster patients, and the new operations manager is working on improving pricing and coding with the help of a consultant.

Developing Information Systems

Metro is making a big transition to more modern systems. Previously, individual departments had their own information systems. They are now installing an integrated system (except for inpatient care) that will cost $20 million over the next three years. The Information Systems Committee started out searching for a purely clinical system and instead replaced a number of systems, looking for one vendor to replace the paper records. They chose Epic Systems as the new vendor because its system included scheduling for physicians and ancillaries, professional billing, managed care referrals and authorizations, and an electronic medical record.

The new system was justified on financial terms to the Metro board, based on labor savings. But the new system will also be more accurate, produce information in a timelier way, help Metro satisfy external data requirements, and provide clinical decision support. An intensive training program will have to be conducted for physicians, who have recently been surveyed. According to Dr. Estes, most physicians have some experience with information systems and are not opposed to implementing the new system.

Measuring Quality, Improving Outcomes, and Increasing Patient Satisfaction

Metro is part of the Cleveland Health Quality Choice outcomes-measurement program, in which hospitals play a more active role in managing length of stay. As a result of government mandate, attending physicians must be personally involved in care, so Metro has transitioned from a resident-based to an attending-driven model.

Metro has a quality department and a case-management department that do concurrent quality and financial reviews of patient stay. Quality and utilization committees collect this data and then share it with the relevant department. If multiple departments are involved, the physician in charge of quality improvement addresses the issue. For example, one such issue was communication of abnormal findings in x-ray. Radiologists didn't call the requesting doctor in all cases. The quality department did a root case analysis of the problems. Now physician-to-physician verbal communication is required to close a radiology file. Metro has an open communication system regarding errors, and the Quality Improvement Committee looks at how to improve the processes. For example, patients receiving anti-coagulation medicine were being dosed too heavily and the process was not being monitored carefully enough. An interdisciplinary initiative was launched and three to four protocols were reduced to two with a single pharmacy-based mixture instead of one mixed by a nurse according to physician order.

The director of the quality department spends 10 percent of his time on this function and there are 12 FTEs in the quality department. Case management has 35 to 40 FTEs. Each year the Quality Improvement Steering Committee reviews the prior year's accomplishment and has a prioritization session for the next year (see Appendix 9.2 for Quality Improvement Steering Committee minutes, 1998 Performance Improvement Selection grid, Performance Improvement Initiatives 1998 and 1999, and Quality Improvement Report Schedule). The top quality improvement priority last year was customer service, specifically, and developing an organizational culture to support customer service. Next year the committee is planning to focus on improving emergency department throughput.

The quality department reviews medical records to meet managed care requirements and reviews ambulatory care charts quarterly. An ombudsman directs complaints to supervisory staff for response. The most frequent complaint was rudeness by employees, which led to the customer service program.

Physician leadership is directly involved in improving patient satisfaction. For example, the new chief of pediatrics found long waits and dissatisfaction in the clinics, with idle time in the morning and overcrowding in the afternoons. Residents were canceling sessions to take elective courses. Now after residents schedule sessions, they can be canceled only 45 days in advance. The number of schedulers was increased and they were moved to the patient care area. A nurse advice line was installed, which improved service to patients regarding prescription refills. As a result of improved scheduling, more pediatric services are provided by appointment rather than as walk-ins. The chief is now working on extending hours of operation in evenings and on Saturdays. He says, "I've had administrative support. I have faculty support to do what is good for the patient. We are not compromising education. I lead by example, doing clinics myself, and once a month being on inpatient service. So I know what the problems are."

The Role of Medical Leadership

In addition to being chief of staff, Dr. Melinda Estes is the senior vice president for medical affairs. Dr. Estes has worked in the Cleveland market for 15 years, and has been at Metro for two. (See Illustration 9.6 for an organizational chart of the department of medical affairs). She is supported by four associate chiefs of staff in the following areas: inpatient services, ambulatory care, managed care and utilization, and professional staff affairs. Only four of the chairs who were there when she was hired remain two years later.

In 1997, Dr. Estes found that the quality of physicians was excellent but many had a "victim mentality." Data for effective management was lacking. "We didn't know who we were admitting, how long they were staying, who was taking care of them, and how well we were billing. We had the information somewhere, but not in usable form." Multiple decision-making groups were meeting in parallel fashion, including the multispecialty group practice, the faculty business office, and the physician-hospital organization. The physicians were not taking responsibility for making decisions.

Department chairs, always key leaders at Metro, are now leaders of the institution as well. The new philosophy is (1) departmental business is everyone's business; (2) the office of medical affairs is looking at what departments are doing; (3) the leadership is to deliver bad news

ILLUSTRATION 9.6

The MetroHealth System Department of Medical Affairs

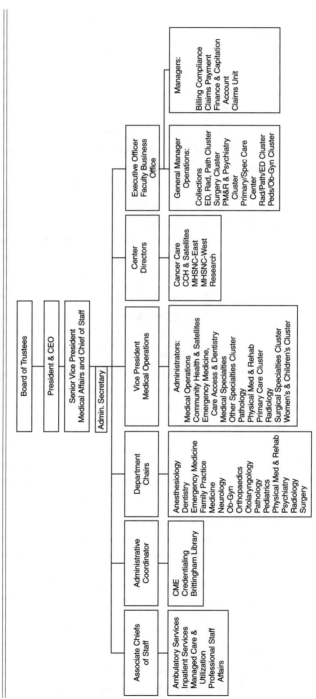

without blaming scapegoats; (4) department chairs understand and craft the institutional vision, and must buy into and sell that vision; and (5) department chairs must understand their business—operationally, fiscally, and strategically. Dr. Estes has begun to set clear expectations. For example, when she came, "no one would send anyone they knew" to the department of dentistry. The area was physically dirty, faculty providers rarely, if ever, provided care, the support personnel were rude and unhelpful, little attention was paid to billing, revenue collections were low, it was a 9 to 3 operation, and their phone abandonment rate (callers hanging up when no one answered) was 70 percent. Dr. Estes reviewed performance with the chair and set expectations using MGMA standards for benchmarking, as adapted by standards at the dental school. She set modest expectations, moving from three to five patients per dentist during a four-hour shift. There was no progress over six weeks. She was visited by two young faculty dentists who said they could "clean matters up." She shared their recommendations with the chair, who replied that the department was functioning optimally and that Dr. Estes didn't understand dentistry. She asked him to step down as the chair. An interim chair was appointed and dentistry is now one of Metro's most productive, respected, and profitable departments. Metro employees now use it. This was accomplished over 12 to 14 months, with a unionized workforce.

The medical operations group provides support to the departmental chairs. Between 75 and 80 persons work in this group, which serves as the administrative side for the medical groups. Previously these staff had worked in the individual departments. The group has seven cluster departments for administrative purposes, each headed by an administrator. These staff changes were made in a budget-neutral manner.

Dr. Estes chairs the MetroHealth Management Council (MMC). This group makes policy, develops strategy, and has fiscal responsibility. The MMC has seven physicians and three hospital managers (the CEO, the chief financial officer, and the chief nursing officer). The vice president for medical operations provides administrative support and is a nonvoting member. The president of the medical staff is ex officio. (They have never had to take a vote.) Dr. Estes selected a balance of primary care and specialty care physicians to serve on this committee, all acknowledged leaders who could think institutionally. The chiefs of surgery and medicine are on the MMC, as are the chief of radiology, the chair of pediatrics, the chair of ob-gyn, the director of community health, and the director of ambulatory care. There are two women.

Since August 1997, the MMC has had three all-day retreats, the last one addressing educational affiliations: what to get from them, and how to renegotiate affiliation contracts. The CMO sets the agenda for MMC meetings. After each meeting, executive summaries are sent to the department chairs. These summaries are discussed at monthly medical staff meetings and by the medical executive committee. Dr. Estes attends departmental meetings, as invited, at least once a year. She holds quarterly lunches with 12 different physicians whom she usually doesn't otherwise see, and walks around and tours departments by design. She writes 15 to 20 personal notes a week to physicians recognizing service or effort and communicates with physicians by e-mail and by appointment. Dr. Estes believes that to be effective, the physician leader must communicate, communicate, communicate, be a problem solver, and be proactive in leading change.

Note

1. Community Report Cleveland Ohio, Fall 1998, Center for Studying Health System Change, Washington, DC.

APPENDIX 9.1
MetroHealth Management Council Protocol

Vision

The MetroHealth Management Council ("MMC") will play a key leadership role in establishing and maintaining the MetroHealth System ("MHS") as a highly competitive, cost-effective and compassionate provider of improved healthcare to the Cuyahoga County and Northern Ohio community. This will be accomplished in a setting that continues to support health education and research.

Mission

The MMC will define and oversee the implementation and evaluation of MHS healthcare initiatives including strategic, financial and operational practices. It will also develop and maintain an effective partnership between healthcare provider and hospital economies.

Objectives

Activities of the MMC will be consistent with the established vision and mission and will focus on:

1. Definition of strategic business opportunities, ventures and partnerships.

2. Identification and prioritization of opportunities that will lead to cost and operational improvements.
   • Set priorities for the allocation of resources.
   • Review and approve budgets.

3. Initiation and oversight of ad-hoc committees established to analyze operational change, develop market opportunities and prepare business plans for recommendation to the MMC.
   • The MMC will define the initial mission, objective and charge for ad-hoc committees. This may be subsequently refined by the Ad-hoc Committees and approved by the Management Council.

Committee Composition

The MMC will be chaired by the Sr. Vice President and Chief of Staff and will be composed of seven physician staff, the President of the Medical Staff, and three Hospital representatives.

As of July 24, 1997, members of the MMC are:

MMC Members:

Melinda Estes, MD Chair	Mark Malangoni, MD
Terry White	Chris McHenry, MD
Errol Bellon, MD	Les Nash, MD
Roxia Boykin, RN	Greg Norris, MD
Pat Catalano, MD	Richard Olds, MD
Ann Harsh	Harry Walker, MD

Governance & Process

The Chairperson of the MMC is responsible for setting the agenda for each meeting. Other processes will function as detailed below and as graphically illustrated.

A. *Member Terms*
   a) The Senior Vice President for Medical Affairs will chair the MMC.
   b) The Chief Executive Officer, Chief Financial Officer, Vice President for Patient Care Services and the President of the Medical Staff will be permanent members of the council.
   c) The chairperson annually at the first meeting of the MMC in July will appoint all Council members, excluding those indicated in b) above.
   d) Members are expected to attend all council meetings and the attendance of alternates will not be allowed.

B. *Reporting*
   a) The MMC will report through the CEO to the Board of Trustees.

C. *Communication of MMC Meetings and Activities*
   An objective of the Council is to communicate their activities to all levels of the organization. The Council will communicate through a single out-going communication that will be in the form of an executive summary. Other forums of communication will include:

   • MHS Medical Leadership Council
   • MEC
   • Department Meetings
   • Town Hall Meetings
   • Management Meetings

   Minutes will be maintained for the use of the Council.

   Communication from MHS staff to the MMC should flow through the members of the Council with any MHS staff having the opportunity to communicate to the Council.

D. *Committee Meeting Process*
   a) An Executive Session will be used for sensitive issues as determined by the chairperson.
   a) Reports of Other Committees.

Formation and Process for Standing and Ad-hoc Work Groups and Task Forces

The Chairperson of the MMC is responsible for establishing standing and ad-hoc work groups and task forces, assigning a chairperson for the committee and identifying an initial charge and focus for the work groups or task forces. In the case where a member of an ad-hoc work group or task force is not a member of the MMC, the MMC Chair will assign a member of the MMC to be the primary interface to the ad-hoc work group or task force chair.

Communication through an MMC Council representative is designed to ensure consistent communication and to facilitate requests for information or other resources that may be required by the work groups or task forces. The MMC will set standard of performance for the work groups or task forces and will monitor and adjust implementation strategies as necessary.

A. *Responsibilities of Ad-Hoc Work Groups and Task Forces Chairs*
   a) Communicate and refine the work groups or task forces mission and charge with members.
   b) Assure that a meeting schedule is established and meetings are held.
   c) Assure that minutes are recorded.
   d) Work with group to establish list of deliverables and time frames.
   e) Apprise the MMC of critical issues and report to Management Council as requested by the Management Council.

B. *Evaluation of Work Groups and Task Forces Rcommendations:*
   The MMC will evaluate all work groups and task forces recommendations. Once these recommendations and plans are accepted by the MMC, the designated representative will be assigned for oversight of implementation.

APPENDIX 9.1
Graphical Representation of MMC Decision Process

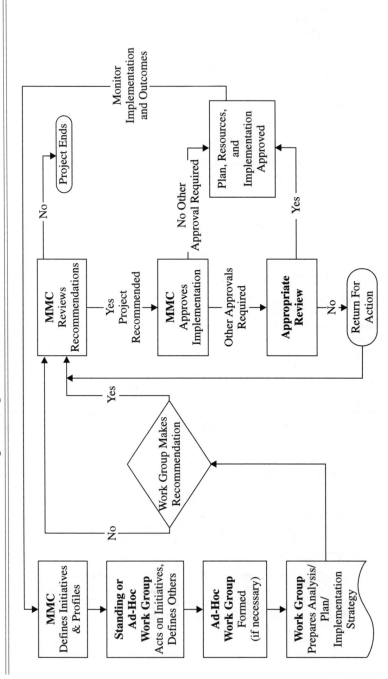

MetroHealth System Quality Improvement Steering Committee

MetroHealth System Quality Improvement Steering Committee	1/21/99 1:00 PM - 2:30 PM K-101 ← NOTE: Change in Location for 1999 Meetings

Meeting Called by:	Brendan Patterson, MD		

Attendees:	S. Amin	M. Legerski	J. Schlesinger
	B. Averbook, MD	T. Lukens, MD	D. Smith, MD
	R. Boykin	M. Malangoni, MD	J. Tomashefski, MD
	B. Brouhard, MD	R. Olds, MD	W. West
	R. Blinkhorn, MD	A. Petrulis, MD	T. R. White

Please Bring: *Minutes, Agenda, Attachments*

AGENDA

	TOPIC	PRESENTER	TIME
1.	Approval of minutes - November 19, 1998		2
2.	Tentative Report Schedule - 1999 (Attachment A)	B. Patterson, MD	5
3.	Brainstorming & Multi-voting - PI Priorities for 1999 (See 1998 Priorities - Attachment B)	Group	30
4.	Evaluation of Program - 1998 (Attachment C)	S. Amin	5
5.	ORYX • Indicator Selection • Data 3rd Q 1998 (Attachment D)	R. Boykin S. Amin	5
6.	P & T Report	B. Averbook, MD	5
7.	Ethics Report	D. Smith, MD	5

APPENDIX 9.2
MetroHealth System 1999 Quality Improvement
Steering Committee Report Schedule*

Reports/ Discussion Topics	Frequency per Year	1/21/99	3/25/99	5/27/99	7/22/99	9/23/99	11/18/99
Benchmark Data							
• Cleveland Health Quality Choice Reports	x2			X			X
• ORYX Data	x2	X			X		
• Anthem Report Card	x1				X		
Accreditation Committee	PRN						
Customer Service Performance Improvement Team	x2			X			X
Ethics Reports	x2	X			X		
External Request Oversight Activities	PRN						
Infection Control Reports	x2		X			X	
Mortality Summary	x1			X			
P&T Reports	x2	X			X		
Pathology Quality	x2		X			X	
Risk Management Reports	x3		X		X		X
Safety Report	x4		4th	1st		2nd	3rd
Transfusion Review Summary (include as part of Pathology Quality Report in 1999)	x1						
Utilization Management Reports	x2		X			X	
PI Priorities	x1 & PRN	X					
Evaluation of Program	x1	X					
QI Plan Review	x1	X					
Plan for Next Year	x1						X
PI Initiative Updates	PRN						
New Business	PRN						
Total # Scheduled Reports		6	5	4	5	4	5

*Note: If emergency discussion/actions required when regular report is not scheduled, add as an agenda item under new business.

APPENDIX 9.2
MetroHealth System 1998 Performance Improvement Selection Grid

Selection Criteria (factors considered during brainstorming & multi-voting processes)	
A. Accomplish mission & goals; actualize vision (Strategic Priorities 1-7)	
B. Hospital-wide function not currently being assessed (Strat. Pr. 2,4,7)	Potential projects identified by MHSQISC members during brainstorming session (February 1998)
C. Current or previous compliance issue (Strategic Priorities (1,4,7)	
D. UR, RM, QC, Infection Control issue (Strategic Priorities (1–3)	
E. High cost or significant savings potential (Strategic Priorities 3)	
F. Benchmarking information available (Strategic Priorities 4,7)	
G. Evidence of variations in practice (Strategic Priorities 1,4)	
H. External customer expectation/need (Strat. Pr. 1,5)	
I. New process or problem-prone activity (Strat. Pr. 2,4,7)	
J. Strong internal interest (Strategic Priorities 1–7)	
K. High Volume	MULTIVOTING RESULTS*
L. High risk	(3 points if selected as highest priority
Total Points	1 point if 3rd highest priority
Potential Projects	0 points if not selected as one of the top 3 choices)
Customer Service (Int. & Ext.)	23 points
Error Management/Root Cause	14 points
Specific Disease Management	12 points
Ambulatory Operations	7 points
PreSurgical Evaluation	5 points
Abnormal Labs/communication	3 points
Billing Issues	2 points
Surgical Waiting Area	0 points
Transportation/East Side	0 points
ORYX/SB50/Sentinel Events	
JCAHO	

CONFIDENTIAL/QA PURPOSES   *Based on responses from 11 individuals

APPENDIX 9.2

MetroHealth System Quality Improvement Steering Committee
Performance Improvement Initiatives - 1998*

Committee Oversight Activities
- Set performance improvement priorities for 1998 (2/98, 4/98)
- Restructured committee membership and reporting relationships (4/98)
- Developed tentative reporting structure for activities in 1999 (11/98)

Customer Service
- Developed an improvement team to address customer service issues (2/98)
- Identified key deliverables (7/98)
- Developed timeline to accomplish identified strategies/tasks (9/98)

Data Review
- Cleveland Health Quality Choice (4/98, 6/98, 11/98)
- Mortality summary data (5/98)
- Transfusion appropriateness data (5/98)
- ORYX indicators (11/98)

Ethics Committee
- Provided several patient care consultations (9/98)
- Participated in ethics-related educational activities (9/98)
- Discussed/made recommendations regarding ethical concerns of "Do-Not-Resuscitate" policies/procedure, informed consent, advance-directives, managed care

Joint Commission
- Notified that the Joint Commission Type I Recommendations were addressed satisfactorily (2/98) & of revised Joint Commission grid score (4/98)
- Had a Mock Joint Commission Survey by a consulting team (7/98)
- Received results of Mock Survey & developed action plan (9/98)

Infection Control Committee
- Summarized reorganization activities of Employee Health program (9/98)
- Reviewed data regarding care of inpatients with pulmonary tuberculosis in 1997 (9/98)

Informed Consent
- Formed a sub-committee to address informed consent issues (5/98)
- Identified methods to document informed consent (7/98)
- Identified educational needs (7/98)
- Classified major vs. minor procedures needing informed consent (11/98)

Managed Care
- Anthem
  - Notified that actions taken in response to 1996 Report Card were accepted (2/98)
  - Collected & submitted required data for 1997 (4/98)
  - Notified of passing 1997 Report Card score (5/98)
  - Collected & submitted required data for 1st half 1998 (11/98)
- Cleveland Health Network
  - Provided results of medical record audits, office site reviews, & long term care site review (5/98)
- Explored alternative methodologies for conducting required medical record audits & office site reviews (7/98)

Pathology Quality Committee
- Implemented new reporting structure for related committee activities (Tissue Committee, Transfusion Committee, Point of Care Testing Committee & Departmental QI Committee) (9/98)
- Evaluated the performance of INR testing in a proposed Anticoagulation Clinic (9/98)
- Implemented efforts to reduce wastage of fresh frozen plasma & platelets (9/98)
- Implemented a new mechanism to improve turnaround time for specific test results in pediatrics (9/98)

Pharmacy & Therapeutics Committee
- Revised restriction policy for pharmaceutical representatives
- Implemented corrective actions relative to administration of heparin (11/98)

Risk Management
- Coordinated activities to:
  - Reduce frequency and severity of patient falls (4/98, 7/98, 11/98)
  - Reduce elopements from the Emergency Department (4/98)
- Conducted critical incident reviews with corrective actions for:
  - Administration of heparin (4/98, 7/98, 11/98)
  - Antibiotic administration in the Operating Room (5/98)
  - Administration of conscious sedation (7/98)
- Clarified appropriate use of terms "sentinel events" and "critical incidents" (7/98)
- Shared plans for a "Mock Trial" educational session in 1/99 (11/98)

Safety
- Reviewed the annual summary of activities for all Environment of Care components (4/98)
- Summarized capital expenditures to remove physical barriers & improve ADA compliance (5/98, 11/98)
- Noted activities aimed at reducing employee injuries (5/98, 7/98, 11/98) & exposure to latex products (7/98)
- Clarified staff roles regarding the use of restraints in conjunction with patient care (5/98)
- Noted reduction in general liability claims due to efforts by Facilities Engineering to correct hazards on grounds & by Logistics Department to train staff in safe/defensive driving (5/98)
  - Training of staff (5/98)
  - Revision of emergency preparedness & disaster planning (7/98, 11/98)
- Shared activities to integrate Life Flight safety into general safety activities (5/98) and results of inspection of the helipad by the Cleveland Fire Department (11/98)
- Summarized activities taken to improve safety within the physical plant (7/98, 11/98)
- Addressed storage practices in the Quad & the basement of Bell Greve buildings (7/98)
- Noted results of inspection by State of Ohio OSHA that was conducted in response to an employee complaint regarding air quality in the Quad (7/98, 11/98)

Utilization Management
- Provided denial data for delegated utilization management plans (11/98)

---

*As documented in 1999 minutes from MetroHealth System Quality Improvement Steering Committee

Case 10

The Primary Care Instrument Panel at Central Community Health Plan

Duncan Neuhauser

Two student teams are doing a field elective project under the supervision of Peter Alexander, M.D., who is chief medical officer and chief operating officer of Central Community Health Plan (CCHP). Central Community is a managed care plan with 500,000 enrollees in an area with a population of 2.5 million people and is by far the largest health plan in the area.

The teams each include a medical student, nursing student, and health management student, all of whom are enrolled in an interdisciplinary course on continuous quality improvement (CQI) in healthcare. The teams are expected to work on a problem assigned to them: to understand the process and causes of variation, and to plan an improvement to this process.

Dr. Alexander finished his residency in general internal medicine the week before he started this job at Central Community Health Plan (CCHP), turning down several similar positions to accept this one. Before starting his residency, he worked for the Hospital Corporation of America. He did his residency on a half-time basis. While doing so, he developed a successful consulting company advising physician groups about managed care.

Peter: CCHP now contracts with 3,000 independent providers who are mostly physicians in our service area. We have contracts with 22 hospitals in the area, which account for about a third of the total in the area. These contracted hospitals agree to provide care at low prices and to participate in utilization review, and have reputations for good care. The physicians also have contracts defining the prices they charge for services and agreeing to utilization review. CCHP has revenue and expenses of about $2 billion a year.

Student: All over town, hospitals and physician groups are being purchased and grouped together as systems of care competing with each other. Do you plan to do this?

Peter: We have three choices. First, we could buy hospitals, group practices, nursing homes, pharmacies, home care organizations, and such. A lot of capital would be tied up in this approach, but we would have more direct control.

Our second choice is to buy nothing, but contract with independent physicians, hospitals, and other providers. In this case, our organization will be small in staff. I envision a corporate headquarters of about 50 people for this $2 billion to $3 billion corporation. Our corporate staff will consist of physicians, practice management consultants, management information system managers, quality improvement coaches, and people who write contracts with providers and employer groups. The value added, based on the relatively small capital invested (compared to owning hospitals), would be great.

The third choice would be a mix of one and two. If the opportunity or need arose to own a provider corporation, we could buy it. We would take a mixed approach, depending on the circumstances. Of these three, we are taking the second approach for now.

Student: Is this wise? Why wouldn't the providers create their own managed care plan and go directly to the payers, thereby passing CCHP entirely? In a sense, HMOs like Kaiser Permanente do this.

Peter: HMOs like Kaiser Permanente have a different set of strengths and weaknesses and a role to play. We think there is a larger role for a plan like CCHP.

We are planning to select about 800 primary care providers out of our 3,000 providers and to work with them closely. We call this core group our "platinum providers." The 800 physicians are members of 90 group practices. They will have an opportunity to own part of CCHP. We will provide them with expert advice on improving their practice. We will provide an information system in support of their practice, which will have several components. It will eliminate their back office paperwork related to billing. The patient's credit card or CCHP member card "swiped" by a machine reader will bring up the patient's record, record the care provider, and make billing from plan to provider automatic. The patient's self-pay component will be taken care of before the patient leaves the office.

We plan to have a council of expert medical advisers to bring the latest knowledge to our partnership. Our staff is prepared to assess the group's readiness for managed care and to give advice on improving market share, improving office practice, analyzing competitors, and planning. We plan to be able to provide these groups with accounting support, information systems, and group purchasing with the goal of reducing the percentage of the group's income that goes to office expense from the current 55 percent to 35 percent. We plan to have the capacity to develop "clinical profiling" for individual physicians and groups and for all our plan members. These include

1. pathophysiological outcomes (for example, average blood-sugar level for your diabetics);
2. patient satisfaction;
3. functional health status (for example, sickness days);
4. future patient health risk (for example, percent of appropriate patients who have had mammography); and
5. costs to payer of plan—both direct and indirect (for the XYZ corporation, the costs per employee and family member, both medical care costs and other company costs such as sick leave days).

These measures will be the basis for data displayed on our physician instrument panel.

Student: What is an instrument panel?

Peter: It's like flying an airplane. What "real time" information should a primary care provider have to be able to manage his or her practice superbly? Our goal is to have ready access to the information needed to measure costs, quality, and satisfaction for the physician's panel of providers at CCHP. Here is an outline of one (see Illustration 10.1).

Student: Will you pay the doctors more if they have better satisfaction scores than others? Will you punish those with worse scores? I know of a managed care plan where doctors get $10,000 end-of-year bonuses for very satisfied patients and lose $10,000 if their patients are dissatisfied.

Peter: What would be Dr. Edward Deming's answer to that question?

ILLUSTRATION 10.1
Template for an Instrument Panel Displaying Inputs (Patient Case-Mix
Variables), Clinical Process Variables, and Outputs (Clinical Outcomes,
Functional Outcomes, Patient Satisfaction, and Cost and Utilization).

PATIENT CASE-MIX   CLINICAL PROCESSES

Patient Descriptors   Process Variables

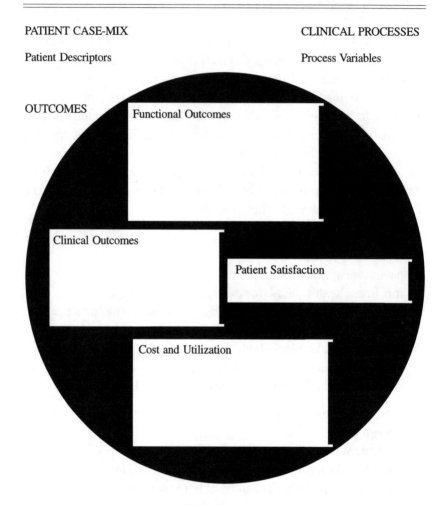

OUTCOMES

Functional Outcomes

Clinical Outcomes

Patient Satisfaction

Cost and Utilization

Our whole idea is to be partners with physicians, not to punish them and
not to own them. They have suffered too much from unthinking, venal
managed care plans. We want to be different.

When we meet next week, I want one student team to present me with
the information that should be in our primary care instrument panel. Here

ILLUSTRATION 10.2
**Basic Statistics for the Total Health Insurance Product (HMO,
Managed Care, Medicaid HMO, Individual Company Plan, etc.)**

Per Member per Month (PMPM); Statistics by Each Provider

- Inpatient days PMPM
- Outpatient days PMPM
- Specialty services PMPM
- Total care PMPM
- Inpatient admissions per 1,000 members
- Inpatient average length of stay
- Paid by plan per inpatient admission
- Paid by plan per inpatient day
- Paid outpatient care claim
- Paid specialty care claim

are some ideas. Illustration 10.2 shows some information that will help us track our comparative costs.

You might also think about the HEDIS measures. As you know, these are the performance measures that employer-payers judge us on. They expect us to have this information. The HEDIS data are changing but will continue to include such measures as (1) the percentage of the elderly who've had influenza immunizations; (2) the percentage of women of the appropriate age ranges who have had a Pap smear and mammography; (3) the percentage of our children who are up-to-date on their immunizations; and (4) how we are doing on our prenatal and well-child visits. Many of our payers will insist on seeing these data.

Here is an example of a reporting form about patient satisfaction generated by a national healthcare marketing research corporation (see Illustration 10.3). The bar graph shows the results of three yearly surveys of member satisfaction for the Alpha Health Plan. Their satisfaction is improving, but tracks at below the average for all plans and is significantly below the best HMO in their market. Perceptions about access to specialty care are going down over time for Alpha Health Plan and are now significantly below the average of all HMOs and worse than the top HMO.

We're also thinking about generating another kind of report from information we can get now from our insurance information system. This physician report would give average information for all the members of the group and for the individual physician. It would show for Dr. Athens'

ILLUSTRATION 10.3
**Alpha Health Plan—Health Plan Report of General Member
Satisfaction, December 1995 (Total Sample N=384)**

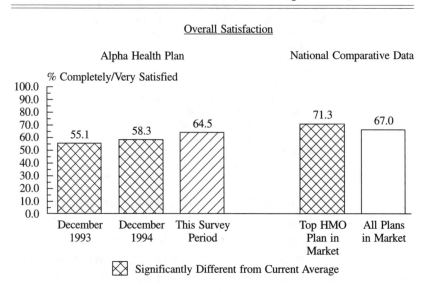

patients their average age, utilization by age, case severity, future risk, payments by diagnostic codes, and utilization over time compared to all the members in our HMO. A map would show the residence of patients coming to the group practice of Dr. Athens. A third report would list procedure codes and her charges to our health plan (see Illustration 10.4). If you look closely, you will see that these numbers are made up, but they give you an idea of what they could look like.

Student: It looks like the doctors are being paid on a fee-for-service basis now rather than capitation. Can you lower costs that way?

Peter: Good question. There are several possibilities. Good physicians are ready to adjust their practice patterns to fit the partnership goals. We can change the payment methods and we would do this in cooperation with our platinum provider partners. With 90 practices, we can do cooperative experimental changes by inviting some groups to change, measuring the results, and then watching to see what happens. The bottom line is that it is in all our interests to prosper and not go out of business.

However, our fee-for-service process is now the way our data are generated. We know who our enrollees are, where they live, and some basic demographics (age, sex, family size). We know the charges sent in by doctors, x-ray, labs, pharmacy, and hospitals linked to the patient and to the patient's primary doctor.

Student: What is a value compass?

Peter: Think of a regular compass. Patient satisfaction is measured in the northern direction, functional status (like average activities of daily living score) is to the west, costs per members per month to the south, and physiologic status to the east. Each of these is scored along each direction. The goal is to be farthest away from the center on all four directions. This form of presentation allows for comparisons with the previous level or with others.

I want one student team to present to me what you think should be the core information for the physician's instrument panel. Be prepared to tell me how it will be collected, how it should be used, and how useful it will be for achieving our goal of excellent care at a reasonable and competitive price.

Here are two more reporting forms I want you to look at. The first is a "spider web diagram" (see Illustration 10.5). Such diagrams can show many performance measures. In this example, each measure is based on a target that becomes 100 percent and the points indicate how closely the group has achieved each goal. In this case, 85 percent of employees are satisfied with their work while 98 percent of outpatients and plan members are satisfied. This example of a spider diagram comes from a large hospital-based system.

The other performance report is from a regional hospital. One of its quality indicators is readmission within 14 days after a prior discharge. This is reported monthly over three years with three sigma upper and lower control limits. If a point is outside these control limits, this would be "out of control." As you can see, the percentage of readmissions is stable at 3 percent over this time with random fluctuation (see Illustration 10.6). The control limits vary with each measure as a result of small changes in the number of admissions per month. What tools would you recommend we use and why?

I have a task for the other student team. As you know, we can't just give out this information and expect it to be used. We are planning an ongoing, continuing medical (and nursing) education program using the

ILLUSTRATION 10.4
A. R. Athens, M.D.: Procedure Codes
Submitted to CCHP, 1/1/96–11/15/96

Description	Number	Total Charges	Average
Office/out PT visit (E&M) estab PT: moderate complexity, 25 min.	187	$12,903	$69
Office consultation new/estab PT: high complexity, 80 min.	55	$11,660	$212
Office/out PT visit (E&M) estab PT: low complexity, 15 min.	222	$11,100	$500
Inj., tendon sheath, ligament/trigger points/ganglion cyst	43	$3,080	$71
Arthrocentesis, aspiration and/or injection; major joint	25	$1,950	$78
Arthrocentesis, aspiration and/or injection; small joint, bursa/ganglion	25	$1,550	$62
Office consultation new/estab PT: moderate complexity, 60 min.	7	$1,246	$178
Office consultation new/estab PT: low complexity, 40 min.	5	$780	$156
Arthrocentesis, aspiration and/or injection; intermed. joint	10	$670	$67
Office/out PT visit (E&M) estab PT: high complexity, 40 min.	5	$640	$128
Office consultation new/estab PT: low severity, 30 min.	5	$580	$116
Injection triamcinolone acetonide, per 10 mg	31	$465	$15
Office/out PT visit (E&M) estab PT: problem/minor 10 min.	7	$287	$41
Immunization, active influenza virus vaccine	12	$180	$15
Administration of influenza virus vaccine	9	$90	$10
Incision & drainage of abscess; simple or single	1	$70	$70
Office/out PT visit (E&M) established PT: minimal, 5min.	2	$68	$34
Methotrexate sodium, 50 mg	1	$23	$23
Injection, vitamin B-12 cyanocobalamin, up to 1000 mcg	2	$22	$11
		$47,364	

method of academic detailing. To start, when a group practice is ready
to have a third individual and comparative practice data printout, one
of our central office physicians and administrative staff will visit their
plan to review their own information. We expect they will be interested
in learning and improving in one or more of their care dimensions. We
must be prepared to respond "just in time" to this perceived need with

ILLUSTRATION 10.5
Lutheran Medical Center Performance Report

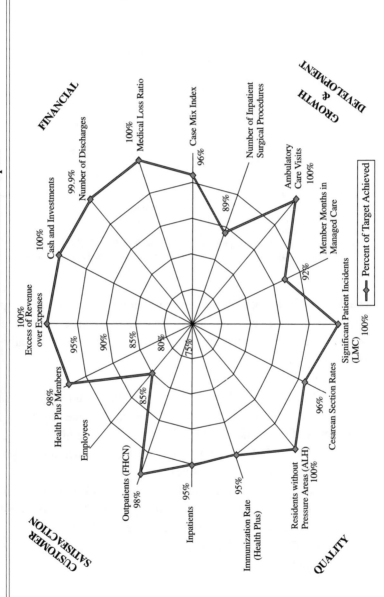

ILLUSTRATION 10.6
Readmissions Within 14 Days of Prior Discharge 1995–1996

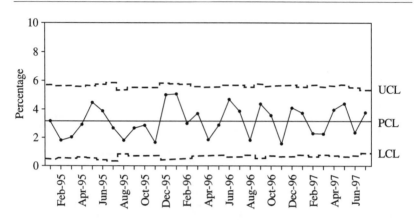

UCL = Upper Control Limit (+3 Sigma), LCL = Lower Control Limit (0)
Indicator: Re-admissions within 14 days of prior discharge
Numerator: The number of patients readmitted
Denominator: Patients admitted to ANMC
Dimension(s) of Performance: Appropriateness, Continuity, Effectiveness, Efficacy
Analysis: Chart displays normal variation. Control limits recalculated as of June 1997.

a package of learning material (articles, audiotapes, videotapes, special consultation, seminars, or whatever learning modality they prefer). If they want to improve patient satisfaction, we need to be ready with immediate practical answers.

Student: What is academic detailing?

Peter: It's the same idea as a drug company detail selling, where a representative goes to the doctor's office to educate the physician about the benefits of his or her company's product. Academic detailing uses the same method, but sends out academic health center staff to provide education about good care practices.

I want the second student team to report back next week on the educational topics we need to have ready to go. Bring me a list and be prepared to explain the reasons for inclusion. You might even draft a full outline of a top-priority topic.

See you next week.

Short Case G

Working with Doctors at Suburban Community Hospital

Anthony R. Kovner

You are the board of Suburban Community Hospital. Your hospital has an excellent reputation in the community. In your target area, 60 percent of the area residents are admitted to Suburban Community and 40 percent are admitted to other nearby hospitals. Eighty-five percent of your admissions are from your target community. A number of large HMOs have been formed in your state, and large insurance companies have been developing point-of-service plans, involving the creation of provider networks. Your hospital, with other hospitals, has set up a large PPO and you are a participating provider in about 20 insurance plan networks.

Your CEO has informed you that the hospital's environment is forecasted to becoming increasingly problematic. Hospital utilization is expected to decrease substantially, as well as utilization of specialists. The trend is for large insurance companies to become increasingly selective regarding which hospitals and specialists participate in their provider networks. Many of the specialists on your medical staff are opposed to any plan in which hospital involvement would mean that all specialists could not participate. In neighboring states, primary care physicians are increasingly recruited by out-of-area hospitals into networks through which they hope to gain specialty referrals. This has not yet happened in your community.

A prestigious outside consultant has recommended to the board that the hospital move proactively with its medical staff in a partnership arrangement in which some part of the medical staff would organize itself into a foundation, a staff model, or an equity model. The advantages of these models are (1) the strength of the tie between primary care physicians and the system; (2) alignment of physician provider interests to promote clinical efficiency; (3) positioning for the future ambulatory growth in healthcare; and (4) joint sharing of risk between the hospital and the physicians.

Your CEO agrees with the consultant concerning the long-range future and about what the hospital should attempt to bring about with its medical staff. However, he suggests that the time is not now right to make any major steps other than what the hospital is already engaged in—contracts as a participating provider with numerous insurance companies and formation of the PPO with other hospitals and their medical staff.

Case Questions

1. Should the hospital be doing anything else at this point to improve its future chances to maintain its present market standing?
2. To what extent should the hospital and physicians be sharing risk, and what alternative relationships are acceptable to the board?
3. Under what circumstances should the hospital attempt to move more quickly and more decisively toward cooperative contracting relationships with only selected members of the specialist medical staff?
4. What data does the board require that it currently does not have to make better decisions in this area?

Short Case H | Complaining Doctor and Ambulatory Care

Anthony R. Kovner

You are the assistant director for ambulatory services. An attending physician complains, "The clerks are no good in this clinic, and neither is the director of nursing." What do you say to him? Assume that the physician is an important customer.

Later during the week, he is still not satisfied. Now *you* are the problem. What do you do now?

Short Case I | Doctors and the Capital Budget

Anthony R. Kovner

You are the hospital CEO. Doctors on the capital budget committee can't agree on which equipment to recommend for purchase and for how much. They are way over budget. What do you say to them?

Short Case J | Doctors and a New Medical Day Care Program for the Terminally Ill

Anthony R. Kovner

You are the hospital CEO. Medical staff is opposed to the hospital's providing needed day care to the terminally ill, which is forecasted to break even financially. They say this is not what the hospital is supposed to do, and that it will actually or potentially compete with their business. What do you say to them?

Short Case K

Average Length of Stay

Anthony R. Kovner

You are the hospital CEO. Two of the doctors consistently keep too many of their patients in the hospital longer than the average LOS for several DRGs. They say their patients are older and sicker and that they're practicing higher quality medicine. What do you say to them?

Part V

Adaptation

Introduction

Adaptive capability involves organizational response to new conditions. Organizations must be innovative or proactive in responding to the pressures of competitors and regulators and to the expectations of various stakeholder groups, from customers to physicians. One indicator of adaptive capability is the presence of specialized units to carry out functions, such as strategic planning and marketing, that are concerned specifically with and held accountable for the adapting function.

Strategic planning can be conducted as a special unit, as part of a specialized unit, by management, or by some combination of the above and is an important area of managerial contribution. Top management sees to it that information is gathered and arrayed regarding the basic businesses of the organization. What is the current mission, nature of the services provided, nature of the population served and targeted to be served, the organization's competitive situation, and what are perceived obstacles to and opportunities for accomplishing current strategy to meet current objectives?

Milio reminds us that organizations have limited problem-solving capacities, wish to avoid uncertainty by arranging negotiated environments, engage in problematic or biased searches for ways of adapting, act on the basis of limited knowledge, and select alternatives on the basis of past successes.[1]

Obviously, decisions to adapt can be the wrong ones relative to organizational goal attainment and system maintenance. Even if the decisions can be shown, in hindsight, to have been technically appropriate, they may have been politically inappropriate. Managers may fail to integrate values of important stakeholders on those directions toward which the organization should focus effort to attain current mission and strategy. We are assuming, of course, that the healthcare organization already has a carefully worked out mission and strategy, one which it is constantly reassessing in terms of competitive and regulatory pressures and in terms of the preferences and expectations of stakeholders, such as physicians and nurses.

Changes in goal direction must often, of political necessity, be gradual or small. Otherwise, important participants who are opposed to such change may withhold their contributions. In a crisis, or at critical decision points involving major changes in organizational mission, such withdrawal may be an acceptable cost, provided that replacement participants are available who are willing and able to make the necessary contributions to organizational goal attainment and system maintenance.

Marketing is important in helping the organizations provide more of what customers and potential customers want and less of what they don't want. Marketing to front-line staff, such as doctors and nurses, is also important because keeping and gaining market share primarily depends on how these staff members manage their performances to elicit customer preference and loyalty.

Circa 2000, healthcare managers are questioning the success of mergers in containing costs, increasing leverage with insurers, and increasing volume. Even as new consolidations are being planned and consummated, other mergers are falling apart. Larger organizations are better able to afford specialized units or departments to gather and array evidence regarding best management practices. Top management's job is to review current mission and strategies and question whether to reallocate scarce resources to pursue a set of strategies; to include providing comprehensive or low-cost services or being a niche player or specialty service provider; and whether to pursue or withdraw as an organization from alliances on what basis with current collaborators and competitors.

The two case studies in this section deal with questions of partnership and alliances and with changes in product focus and delivery. How these questions are answered and what strategies are selected may have consequences that are different for specific organizations and for specific managers. In the case of "The VNA of Cleveland," the CEO, Mary Lou Stricklin, is faced with a set of choices involving new relationships with local collaborators and competitors, some of whom may be seen by some VNA stakeholder groups as threatening the core values upon which the organization was founded and has thrived for many years.

Similarly, Geraldine Patton, the CEO of the West Peoria Veterans Affairs Medical Center, must decide how her center should relate to managed care and to other VA facilities in the region. A task force has recommended that 8,000 patients be initially enrolled in the VA Community Integrated Service Network. A marketing plan that includes the endorsement of veterans service organizations may be undertaken to enroll veterans not currently using the VA, with the inclusion of new (and less seriously ill) patients being seen as critical to success. Other options are suggested, and the CEO must examine critically the assumptions underlying the three different points of view.

Case Questions

The VNA of Cleveland

1. In which direction should the VNA go?
2. How should the VNA board be brought along to agree with the change recommended?
3. How can staff morale be maintained in the face of uncertainty?
4. Who are the stakeholder groups whose expectations Mary Lou Stricklin must manage to succeed in implementing your recommendations?
5. What are the personal stakes involved for Ms. Stricklin in doing as you suggest? How can she maximize the upside potential and minimize the downside risks for her own career?

In a State of Change

1. What criteria should Geraldine Patton use in choosing strategic options? Why choose these criteria?
2. What are the advantages and disadvantages of each of the three options? How do the options rate on each of the criteria that you recommended?
3. What do you recommend that Ms. Patton do? What is the rationale behind your recommendations?
4. How should Ms. Patton proceed in implementing your recommendations? What measurable objectives are reasonable for your recommendations?
5. What are the personal stakes involved for Ms. Patton in doing as you suggest? How can she maximize the upside potential and minimize the downside risks for her own career?

Note

1. Milio, N. "Health Care Organizations and Innovation," in *Health Services Management: Readings and Commentary*, 2nd Edition, ed. A. R. Kovner and D. Neuhauser (Chicago: Health Administration Press, 1983) pp. 448–64.

Selected Bibliography

Begun, J. W. "Strategic Cycling: Shaking Complacency in Healthcare Strategic Planning," *Journal of Healthcare Management* 44:5, Sept–Oct 1999, 339–351.

Curran, C. R., K. W. Kuhn, N. Miller, A. Skalla, R. D. Thurman, *Shaping an Integrated Delivery Network: Home Care's Role in Improving Service, Outcomes and Profitability*. Chicago: Health Administration Press, 1999.

Evashwick, C. J., *Seamless Connections*, Chicago: American Hospital Publishing, 1997.

Griffith, J. R. "Managing the Transition to Integrated Health Care Organizations," *Frontiers of Health Services Management* 12, no. 4 (Summer 1996): 4–50.

Herzlinger, R. E. *Market-Driven Health Care*. Reading, MA: Addison-Wesley, 1997.

Kizer, K. W. "Health Care, Not Hospitals: Transforming the Veterans' Health Administration," in G.W. Dauphinais and C. Price (eds.) *Straight from the CEO,* New York: Simon and Shuster, 1998, pp. 112–120.

Luke, R. D., J. W. Begun, and S. Walston, "Strategy Making in Health Care Organizations," in S. Shortell and A. Kaluzny (eds.) *Health Care Management: Organization Design and Behavior,* 4th Edition, Albany, NY: Delmar Thomson, 2000, pp. 394–431.

Zajac, E. J., and T. A. D'Aunno, "Managing Strategic Alliances" in *Health Care Management: Organization Design and Behavior*, S. M. Shortell and A. D. Kaluzny (eds.) Albany, NY: Delmar Thomson, 2000, pp. 328–64.

Case 11 | The Visiting Nurse Association of Cleveland

Duncan Neuhauser

Mary Lou Stricklin, MBA, MSN, is chief executive officer of the Visiting Nurse Association of Cleveland (VNA). The home care market continues to change rapidly. Competition, DRG payment, HMO growth, the rising burden of indigent care, hospital-based home care programs, hospice, large growth of demand for home care, the explosion of specialized home care services, and the Medicare Balanced Budget reforms all continue to affect the home care market. These rapid changes have led to a series of corporate reorganizations, and Stricklin is contemplating the next corporate transformation.

The year 2002 will be the 100th anniversary of Cleveland's VNA. Throughout its history, the VNA has employed professional nurses with home care experience to provide care to the residents of the greater Cleveland area, which now has a population of approximately 1.2 million people. The mission and value statements for the VNA are shown in Illustration 11.1.

1902–1980

The VNA remains as it began, an independent not-for-profit organization. Originally, it was supported largely by philanthropic contributions. In the early 1900s, Cleveland received a large immigrant population from Europe and later from the South. Its heavy industry base (steel, machine tools, automobiles) was and is cyclical in its level of activities, fluctuating from high prosperity to slack times with layoffs and unemployment. The relative importance of this heavy industry declined in the late 1970s, resulting in a 10 percent population loss by 1985.

ILLUSTRATION 11.1
Visiting Nurse Association of Cleveland: Mission, Vision, and Values

Mission
To provide innovative, high-quality, and cost-effective community healthcare to all people by
• delivering care that promotes health, independence, and dignity;
• teaching people to care for themselves and each other; and
• providing services to the poor as funds permit.

Vision
• To be the leader in innovative home care.
• To be the standard for quality care.
• To be the leader in community health planning and research.

Values
• We value personal dignity, the importance of integrity, honesty, and compassion.
• We are responsive to the needs of the community and our stakeholders.
• We value quality as a measurable outcome of emerging standards of performance.
• We value education and skill development of staff and clients.

Since then, the population has increased slightly and the economy has changed to services and regional distribution; Cleveland is the location of the corporate headquarters of 27 *Fortune* 500 corporations, resulting in greater economic diversity and less cyclical unemployment. In the early 1990s, the economy was doing a bit better than the national average.

Cleveland still has the highest per capita rate of philanthropic giving of any major city in the United States. The advent of Medicare and Medicaid in 1966 allowed for new revenue and expansion of the VNA. The original VNA board of trustees was largely composed of the wives of community leaders when one of the major board functions was to provide Christmas food baskets for needy patients. By the 1990s, the board was diverse by gender, ethnicity, and professional background.

1980: About the Only Game in Town

The 1980 organization chart of the VNA is shown in Illustration 11.2. The core professional staff consisted of full-time salaried generalist nurses who worked out of four district offices to cover Cleveland and adjacent townships. The center office included administrative staff to coordinate several part-time social workers and physical therapists. Calls requesting care were handled by the district offices where nurses were

ILLUSTRATION 11.2
The Visiting Nurse Association of Cleveland Organization (1980)

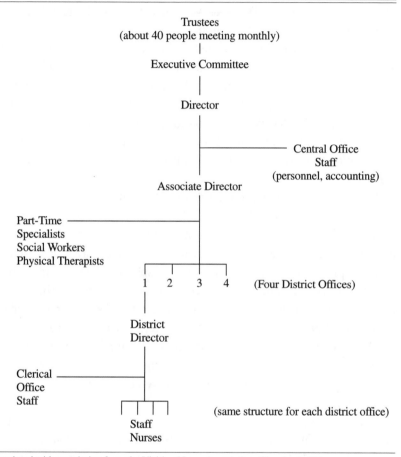

Reprinted with permission from the Visiting Nurse Association, Cleveland, Ohio.

assigned to respond. The nurses themselves decided whether or not a patient was able to pay.

Home care aide services were also provided by the VNA under contract from another voluntary organization, the Center for Human Services. Special contracts provided care for the elderly in several apartment complexes. All services were available during weekday working hours, and the agency was closed on weekends and holidays.

1982: Arrival of Competition

Ohio regulations made it easy to start a home care company, and more than 300 were created. The joke went that if you had a telephone and knew a nurse, you could start a home care agency. If costs could be kept down and full-pay patients selected, home care could be profitable. By 1982, competition for paying home care patients was growing. Others were content to let the VNA provide home care for those who could not pay. In 1984, VNA philanthropic gifts and endowment income yielded $190,000, plus United Way contributions of $540,000, out of a total of $5,000,000 in revenue. This allowed the VNA to provide care to all who requested it. However, the VNA needed mostly paying patients to survive.

This competitive situation led the VNA for the first time to ask the source of its patients and how the choice of home care provider was made. It turned out that 82 percent of patients came by way of hospital discharge and, of these, most came from a dozen of the area's largest hospitals. Typically a nurse, social worker, or discharge planner made the decision within the hospital. The choice of provider depended primarily on agency reputation, the ease of making a referral, and agency name recall.

Instead of being a passive receiver of telephone requests for services, the VNA decided to assign a staff nurse as contact person for each major hospital in addition to regular nursing care activities. Brochures, calendars, and small magnetized VNA symbols were distributed to promote name recognition.

The VNA organized a centralized intake service with one recognizable telephone number as an important step in making referrals easier. At the VNA the belief was that one competitor was giving away transistor radios to hospital-based referrers. After some discussion, the VNA decided not to follow suit.

By 1983, DRG payments had drastically shortened patient stay and emptied hospital beds. Now the hospitals were encouraging earlier discharge combined with home care. Hospitals began actively looking for new revenue-generating ventures and hospital-based home care became popular. By 1983, there was serious concern that the VNA's work would come to an end, as one hospital after another started its own home care program.

By 1984, a number of hospitals decided not to start their own programs, but rather to develop contracts with the VNA. The market again changed; no longer was it the individual nurse's or social worker's decision, but rather a hospital-based contract. One reason hospital contracting occurred was because hospital management was busy; the managers wanted to avoid a new program and save energy for higher-priority areas. By 1984, the VNA had contracts with eight hospitals, which accounted for about 35 percent of VNA's patients.

Early discharge drove the demand for increasingly complex home care requiring home care nurse specialists in intravenous (IV) management, pediatrics, mental health, hospice care, renal dialysis, and ostomy care, in addition to physical and occupational therapy and social work. This specialization and division of labor created economies of scale in home care. A small suburban hospital with paying patients and undifferentiated home care could prosper with small programs. Larger hospitals with more severely ill patients and high indigent care ratios found VNA contracting a better choice. Hospitals that started their own home care programs were unlikely to sell their program to nearby competing hospitals. Hospital contracts led to 24-hour service availability by the VNA rather than a 9-to-5 weekday organization. Hospitals wanted full-service agencies, so the VNA started homemaker services called "All for You." In response to these changes, the VNA reorganized in 1989.

1990–1999: Prosperity for a While

The single not-for-profit [501(c)(3)] organization became six organizations. See Illustration 11.3.

The large group of trustees was divided into a smaller group of trustees with governance responsibility and a group of overseers—loyal supporters of the VNA with no line authority, but a right to advise and contribute.

In 1990, the VNA organizations numbered five:

1. The bulk of the agencies' work is in VNA Services and within this, Medicare was the largest payer.
2. VNA Care Plus provides home aide assistance on a private basis (cleaning, food preparation, and personal hygienic care).

ILLUSTRATION 11.3
Visiting Nurse Association of Cleveland (2000)

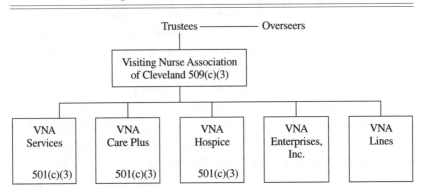

VNA Services

The VNA's full range of services and programs that help petients return to their optimal level of health are available in an eight county area of Northeast Ohio.

- Medical-Surgical Nursing
- Maternal and Infant
- Pediatrics
- Personal Care
- Enterostomal Care
- Older Adult
- Infusion Therapy
- Rehabilitation Services
  - Physical Therapy
  - Occupational Therapy
  - Speech-Language Pathology
  - Social Work
  - Nutrition
- Behavioral Health
  - Mental Health Services
  - Chemical Dependency and Ambulatory Detox
  - AIDS Mental Health
  - Clozaril Treatment
  - Mental Health Management and Support Services

VNA Hospice

VNA Hospice and Special Care are programs for patients who are terminally ill. An interdisciplinary team provides compassionate care including:

- Skilled nursing care
- Pain and symtom management
- Respite care
- 24-hour crisis support
- Social Work services
- AIDS care
- Residential/Nursing Home Care

- Home Care Aides
- Rehabilitation services
- Bereavement support
- Spiritual Care
- Volunteer clergy, lawyers, companions, and Friendly Visitors

VNA Care Plus

VNA Care Plus, formerly All For You, Inc., provides 24-hour private duty nursing and personal care. RN, LPN, aide or homemaker services are available for short-term rehabilitation or long-term supportive care, meal preparation, companionship, respite care and child care.

Services
- Private Duty Nursing
- Personal Care
- Homemaker services

VNA Lines

VNA Lines incorporates nursing, pharmaceutical and supplies services for in-home and nursing home infusion therapy.

- Total Parental Nutrition
- Pain Management Therapy
- Chemotherapy and Antiemetic Therapy
- Antibiotic Therapy
- Cardiac Support Therapies
- AIDS Related Therapies

VNA Enterprises

VNA Enterprises provides an expert team of home healthcare professional who consult nationally and locally in the areas of administration, finance, operations, human resources management, MIS, fund development and program development.

Reprinted with permission from the Visiting Nurse Association, Cleveland, Ohio.

3. VNA Hospice provides care for the terminally ill at home.
4. VNA Enterprises is a small catch-all organization for receiving money for consulting and other services (for profit).
5. VNA Lines provides IV solutions and other supplies needed in home care (for profit).

In the early 1990s, these organizations made surpluses; enough so that, in 1995, the VNA, could, with fundraising, move into a single new modern building in the center of the city near the expressway. By clearly separating out the possible for-profit activities, the nonprofit status of the whole organization could be preserved.

As of 1997, patients cared for by the VNA were paid for as follows: Medicare, 77 percent; Medicaid, 8.7 percent; commercial insurance and Blue Cross, 7.3 percent; other, 5.5 percent; and United Way, 1.5 percent. Reflecting the large Medicare component, most patients are over the age of 65. The VNA has 670 staff (full- and part-time) with a total revenue and expense of about $30 million.

In 1993, projected trends in home care were made with the advice of national consultants. These are shown in Illustration 11.4. As of 2000, the national trend to outpatient care continues. Home care growth, rapid during the 90s, is expected to decline as a result of Medicare payment changes. With respect to technology, VNA nurses are now using laptop computers to collect patient data and manage care. Nearly all VNA nursing care patients are under protocol, and outcome measures are being tracked. Although we are not closer to universal healthcare coverage, locally the consolidation of large delivery systems has occurred.

Mary Lou Stricklin thinks of the VNA as an organized process of care through which patients pass. See Illustration 11.5. This pathway is driven by mission, vision, and values. Patients can be referred from nursing homes, physicians, hospitals, or networks. They proceed through admitting, scheduling, care, and community-based living.

2000

The 40 separate Cleveland area hospitals of 1980 became four competing delivery systems by 1997 and only two by 1999. The two remaining systems are anchored by the Cleveland Clinic Foundation and University Hospitals of Cleveland, which are located a 15-minute walk apart. They have networks of community hospitals, group practices, HMOs, specialty services, and their own in-house home care programs. In 1999, both were losing money.

Medicare, which pays for most home care, saw such expenditures explode in the 1990s and is now attempting to reduce these expenditures through new regulations, including the expected introduction of prospective payment (a fixed total amount per client) rather than payment per visit. This payment method is expected to have as drastic an effect for home care as it did for hospitals. The concern over fraud and abuse in healthcare has led to much more detailed reporting requirements and

ILLUSTRATION 11.4
Projected Industry Trends, 1993

Home Care: Year 2000

Shift to Outpatient Care
Home care will be one of the fastest growing segments of the healthcare industry.
Home care patients will be significantly sicker and require more sophisticated care.
Home care will be an important element of pre- as well as post-acute care of a patient.

Accelerated Impact of Technology
The use of advanced medical technologies in home care will increase significantly.
New drug therapies will significantly change how patients are treated.
The use of computer, communication, and information technologies in home care will
    greatly expand.

Increased Managed Care Penetration
Managed home health care services will be pervasive.
Managed care organizations will have significant control over a patient's choice of
    provider.
Home health services will be carved out for national and regional contracting.
Accreditation, consistency, image, and brand name recognition will be important in
    competing for national/regional contracts.
Case management will play a key role in managed care.
Standard treatment protocols will cover most care.

Demand for Quality/Outcome Measures
Employers and payers will demand quality and outcome measures.
Meaningful quality and outcome measures for home care will be developed.
Quality and outcome measures will be used to select home care providers.

Emphasis on Wellness, Prevention, and a Healthy Lifestyle
Employers/payers will cost-justify wellness programs.
Wellness, prevention, and a healthy lifestyle will be emphasized.
Individuals will be interested and actively involved in their own care.

More Enlightened Public Policy
All citizens will be guaranteed universal access to basic healthcare benefits.
Reimbursement for healthcare services will be fair and equitable.
A "two-tier" healthcare delivery status will be our primary goal.

Emergence of Regional Healthcare Delivery Systems
Integrated healthcare delivery systems offering a full continuum of care will dominate
    local markets.
Collaboration and networking of healthcare organizations will be prevalent.
"Free-standing" healthcare organizations will be rare.

Reprinted with permission from the Visiting Nurse Association, Cleveland, Ohio.

ILLUSTRATION 11.5
1995: The VNA Organization as a Process

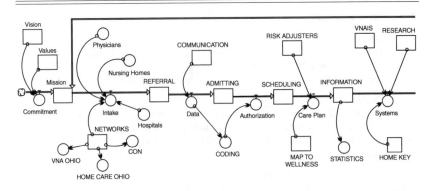

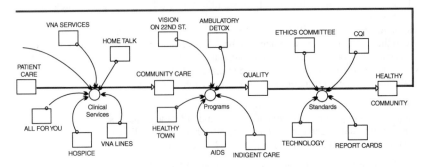

harsh penalties for error, and required a major investment in computer support, including laptop computers for visiting nurses. The VNA is a national leader in this effort to computerize its home care services and has received a written commendation from a federal auditor's site visit inspection.

One consequence of these changes is the closing of small home care agencies across the country. Rumor has it that Medicare officials would be happy to see half the home care agencies in the country go out of business. In the 1990s, everyone was stampeding into home care; now there may be a rush to exit. So far, however, the VNA has been able to adjust to these pressures.

One subcomponent of the VNA is VNA Care Plus, which provides homemaker and home health aide services. These services are in large demand from several different payer sources, including private pay. The problem here is that not enough staff can be found to fill the demand for these services, mainly because of the booming economy. Many jobs are now available for these workers, while reimbursement caps do not allow big pay raises to attract more employees.

In 1997, Mary Lou Stricklin's major strategic question was whether to merge the VNA into a large delivery system, nursing home network, or HMO. A board task force was set up to explore merger possibilities. After two years of work, it was decided to remain independent. As of 2000, the topic was off the table. The two giant local hospital systems have their own home care organizations for their own patients. However, they do not have the United Way support or the endowment support such as the one that allows the VNA to give about one and a half million dollars of free care each year.

If these vertically integrated conglomerates continue as they are, the VNA would have a small role locally in direct home care. A new strategy would be to emphasize the VNA's computer, reporting, and managerial capacity and provide the "back office" support for other home care agencies. It is currently doing this for a piece of one of the local conglomerate's home care organizations.

In business there has been a trend away from "conglomerates" doing business in many markets. Now a new philosophy has emerged popularized by General Electric: Just do what you do best and sell off everything else. The local healthcare is in the conglomerate stage, building vertically integrated systems to maintain the referrals to the big tertiary care hospitals. What if they were to follow the industry by just focusing on tertiary care and spinning off their other parts, including home care? If so, the VNA might be perfectly situated to take over direct home care in Cleveland. Mary Lou Stricklin wonders: Would the VNA have the resources to make such a purchase if it became available?

The VNA has also been expanding beyond the traditional home care activities, including special programs for alcoholism, mental health, and for children. See Illustration 11.6. Community-based health programs such as Healthy Town and Healthy Talk have been developed. The growth of VNA-funded research has been made possible in part by the wealth of care pathway and outcomes data being collected on their own patients and by several other VNAs elsewhere that use the same patient information systems.

ILLUSTRATION 11.6
Visiting Nurse Association of Cleveland

Innovations

Home Talk™
Through a joint venture with Telepractice in the fall of 1995, VNA introduced Home Talk™, a free telephone service for patients that improves access to their VNA clinician. Patients may choose from several options, including an on-line library with recorded health information. Home Talk™ supports the clinician's assessment of a patient's health status resulting in fewer readmissions to the hospital and unnecessary trips to the emergency room.

Ambulatory Detoxification Services
The VNA of Cleveland, Metrohealth, and Alcoholism Services of Cleveland are collaborating on an 18-month demonstration project to provide ambulatory detoxification services and chemical dependency care in home and community settings. This project is funded by a grant from the Cleveland Foundation.

Healthy Town
This program provides health promotion and disease prevention services to lower-income senior citizens and families with children at University Settlement and Collinwood Community Services Center, member organizations of the Neighborhood Centers Association. Funding is provided by the CAVS Charities and the Cleveland Foundation.

HIV/AIDS Mental Health
Through a grant from the AIDS Funding Collaborative, the VNA and the Free Clinic are collaborating to bring nursing care, social work, and consultative services to patients.

KID Connection
KID Connection nurses offer educational programs and consultation services for child care providers. These services help day care staff deliver high-quality care and meet state licensing requirements.

Vision on 22nd Street
To prepare students for community-based nursing, the VNA and Cleveland State University Department of Nursing formed an education-service partnership. A committee of community healthcare experts from both institutions developed new nursing curricula and began offering classes last fall. The program will educate over 200 nursing students within the next few years. Vision on 22nd Street is partially funded by the Cleveland Foundation.

Clozaril Management
Selected patients of the Mental Health program are participating in VNA's collaborative research study, funded by Sandoz Pharmaceuticals, to evaluate the effectiveness of Clozaril, and to implement the program in other areas of the country.

Camp TLC
VNA Hospice's Bereavement Camp TLC, Together Love Continues, is an annual day-long program helping children and family members who have lost a loved one to cope with their grief. The camp is underwritten by the Bicknell Fund.

ILLUSTRATION 11.7
VNA of Cleveland—Current Corporate Operating Structure

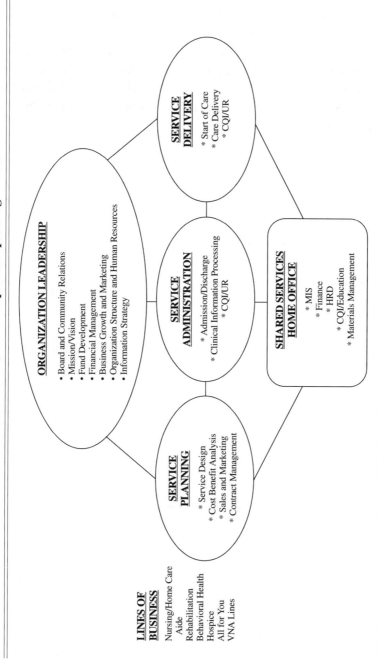

LINES OF BUSINESS

Nursing/Home Care
Aide
Rehabilitation
Behavioral Health
Hospice
All for You
VNA Lines

SERVICE PLANNING

* Service Design
* Cost Benefit Analysis
* Sales and Marketing
* Contract Management

ORGANIZATION LEADERSHIP

• Board and Community Relations
• Mission/Vision
• Fund Development
• Financial Management
• Business Growth and Marketing
• Organization Structure and Human Resources
• Information Strategy

SERVICE ADMINISTRATION

* Admission/Discharge
* Clinical Information Processing
* CQI/UR

SERVICE DELIVERY

* Start of Care
* Care Delivery
* CQI/UR

SHARED SERVICES HOME OFFICE

* MIS
* Finance
* HRD
* CQI/Education
* Materials Management

MIS - Management Information Systems, HRD - Human Resources Development, CQI - Continuous Quality Improvement, UR - Utilization Review

The VNA could expand "horizontally" by moving into smaller cities nearby to provide home care where these services were lost as a result of home care agency closures. Its current corporate structure allows for such expansion. See Illustration 11.7.

Ms. Stricklin realizes that pursuit of these options takes leadership effort and she cannot successfully do them all. How should she prioritize these activities? Which are most important? How can she bring her VNA board along with these changes? How can staff morale be maintained in the face of this uncertainty?

| Case 12 | # In a State of Change: Veterans Affairs and HMOs |

J. J. Donellan, A. R. Kovner,
C. A. Milbrandt, J. Oliveri, B. L. Bell,
D. Anderson, and P. J. O'Neil

The state of West Peoria leads the nation in healthcare reform. In each of the past three legislative sessions comprehensive healthcare reform laws have been passed. The legislation has brought about the following:

- The small employer insurance market has been restructured to enable more citizens to acquire health insurance coverage. Within two years all employers with more than 50 employees will be required to offer and subsidize coverage for employees and their dependents.
- A state-funded health insurance program has been created to cover those citizens who are unable to obtain private insurance and who do not qualify for other government health programs. This program has been in effect for the past year and is offered on a sliding fee basis.
- In three years universal coverage for West Peoria will be implemented. At that time all West Peorians will be required by law to acquire a minimum "basic benefit" package.

With the advent of universal coverage most health providers will organize into integrated service networks (ISNs). Reimbursement rates for providers not participating in an ISN will be regulated by a state-run all-payer system (a modified fee-for-service system) that will severely restrict reimbursement. ISNs will be licensed by the state and will be required to provide, at a minimum, the basic benefit package prescribed by law to anyone wishing to enroll.

Community ISNs (CISNs), a smaller version of an ISN, may begin enrolling patients immediately. Both ISNs and CISNs are required to make primary care services available within 30 miles of an enrollee's home. Secondary and tertiary services (with the exception of highly specialized services such as transplants, open heart surgery, and neurosurgery) must be available within 60 miles of an enrollee's home. Growth in ISN/CISN premium rates will be state regulated, and "report cards" comparing ISN and CISN performance on factors such as cost, quality, and customer satisfaction will be issued annually by the state.

HMOs and managed care plans have been developing in West Peoria since the 1950s. The market is dominated by managed care, with two-thirds of the state's eight million citizens enrolled in some form of managed care plan. Three HMOs now dominate the managed care market, covering 80 percent of the state's managed care enrollees.

Geraldine Patton was recently appointed director of the Dwight D. Eisenhower VA Medical Center in Peoria City (Peoria City VAMC). Patton was assigned to Peoria City by VA Central Office (VACO) for the specific purpose of developing and implementing a transition plan that will ensure VA's success in West Peoria's reformed healthcare market.

Peoria City VAMC is the largest of three VA medical centers in the state and is geographically located near the center of the state. The facility is five years old and is considered by many to be among the finest and most modern of the 170 VA medical centers nationwide. It currently consists of a 500-bed acute care hospital with medical, surgical, rehabilitation medicine, and psychiatric beds, and a 100-bed nursing home. It is a major teaching affiliate of the University of West Peoria Medical School. With the exception of transplantation services, all primary, secondary, and tertiary healthcare services are available at the facility or through a sharing agreement with the university. These include a newly opened women veterans health program and a nationally renowned prosthetic and rehabilitation center. The Medical Center also manages a satellite outpatient clinic located 50 miles to the south of Peoria City. The veteran population of the state of West Peoria is 520,000. Peoria City VAMC treated 38,000 individual veteran patient cases during the past year.

Some management improvements are necessary at Peoria City VAMC. Length of stay for both medicine and surgery is three to five days longer than that found in comparable non-VA community and teaching hospitals. Waiting times for next available appointments are more than

30 days in many of the specialty clinics, and pressure to reduce overall government employment has forced staffing reductions in virtually all departments. A primary care program has recently been instituted, with approximately 25 percent of all outpatients enrolled in this program. Primary care has had a positive effect. Overall, waiting times for next clinic appointments have been reduced, and the satisfaction of patients served by a primary care provider has improved.

Two other VA medical centers are also located in West Peoria. The Lakeland VAMC is located 125 miles to the north of Peoria City, close to the state's northern border. This 150-bed facility offers primary and secondary health services to approximately 12,000 veterans and operates a specialized spinal cord injury program. The Leesville VAMC, located 90 miles to the southeast of Peoria City, operates a 350-bed acute and chronic care psychiatric hospital and a 250-bed nursing home. The hospital specializes in the care of chronic psychiatric patients, with specialized programs of excellence in substance abuse and post-traumatic stress. The nursing home operates at full capacity with a waiting list for admission. A small clinic at Leesville offers primary care services to approximately 10,000 veterans on an outpatient basis. Both the Lakeland and Leesville facilities were built in the 1930s; although some modernization has been done, they are both in need of considerable plant improvements. All three West Peoria VA medical centers are part of a referral network that also includes two VA medical centers in neighboring East Peoria, and one in the state of Tremont, located to the south of West Peoria.

Geraldine Patton appointed a task force from the Peoria City VAMC to analyze the current situation and present an action plan. The task force consisted of the chief of staff, Dr. Urban Grant (chairperson), several medical staff leaders, the associate dean for clinical programs at the University of West Peoria Medical School, the chief of medical administration and fiscal services, and leaders of three different veterans service organizations in the immediate community. Dr. Grant's task force reached consensus on establishing a VA-sponsored CISN based at Peoria City VAMC, with future plans to expand to a statewide ISN in conjunction with the Lakeland and Leesville VAMCs. The report included a financial analysis projecting that a benefit package providing comprehensive coverage meeting state criteria would cost $1,500 per enrollee under age 65, and $5,200 per enrollee age 65 and over (exclusive of supplemental services such as long-term care). For enrolled veterans not living near existing facilities, primary care and emergency services could be offered close to their home by shifting resources to set up multiple community clinics and by establishing contracts with community hospitals and providers.

The task force recommended that 8,000 patients be initially enrolled in the VA CISN; 4,000 should come from Peoria City VAMC's existing patient population, and an additional 4,000 new enrollees should be sought. A marketing plan that included the endorsement of veterans service organizations would be undertaken to enroll veterans not currently using VA. The inclusion of new (and less ill) patients was seen as critical to success; the existing patient base of Peoria City VAMC was disproportionately skewed toward patients with multiple and chronic medical conditions.

The task force also recommended that Peoria City VAMC contract with MetroPru, a large health insurer in West Peoria, to do the actuarial work; to manage enrollment, billings, and collections; and to ensure that equivalent insurance options would be made available as a package to the dependents of veterans who chose to enroll. The cost of contracting with MetroPru to manage the plan was not factored into the report. The task force felt confident that the plan would be competitive in that it would offer health benefits to veterans not customarily available in other CISN/ISN packages (i.e., low-cost prescriptions and broad coverage for psychiatric benefits). Some legislative relief would be necessary, most especially from total employment restrictions. An additional funding stream would also be needed to meet the increased number of patients served. This could be accomplished either by an increase in funding to Peoria City VAMC by VACO based on new enrollment, or through legislative relief permitting Peoria City VAMC to retain insurance collections.

Mrs. Patton discussed the task force recommendations with the directors of the Lakeland and Leesville VAMCs at a network meeting. They were less than enthusiastic. While Peoria City VAMC was well capitalized, the Lakeland and Leesville facilities simply did not have the physical plant and access to staff necessary to compete in the market. They questioned the urgency of such a drastic action, pointing out that many patients already elected to receive care by VA despite having other health insurance, including Medicare. In their opinion, the state reform agenda might in fact create a greater demand for VA care, noting that ISNs would likely exclude coverage of service-connected illness or injury, and offer only very limited psychiatric and long-term care benefits.

They suggested that rather than form an ISN or CISN, the medical centers specifically identify clinical areas of expertise and cost efficiency and aggressively market those services to health insurers. The insurers could purchase these services from VA for eligible veterans enrolled in their plans. They argued that those treatment areas not covered by the required "basic benefit" package where VA had specific expertise, such as prosthetic programs, long-term care, geriatric care, acute and chronic psychiatry, substance abuse, and post-traumatic stress disorder, would become a critical "safety net" for veterans, and an essential ingredient of the state program. Finally, they noted that their strategy would require little action in terms of redirecting resources and facility missions.

Ms. Patton is familiar with another option not yet presented, but one that she was involved in negotiating with the state of Columbia during her last assignment. Rather than trying to initially compete in the market as an insurer, VA could negotiate an arrangement directly with the state, whereby state payments and subsidies would be waived for any care provided to non-service-connected veterans who met VA criteria for mandatory treatment and who elected to receive their care at a VA facility. Through such an arrangement, low-income non-service-connected veterans eligible for state-funded health insurance could receive their care by VA under the auspices of the state plan but at no cost to the state. As category "A" patients, their care would be covered by federal appropriations rather than state payment. This was seen as a win-win arrangement in Columbia. VA gained experience as a provider and administrator of a managed care plan in the early stages of state reform; the state realized savings by avoiding any costs associated with the care of low-income veterans receiving VA care.

Acknowledgments

The authors wish to thank Gary DeGasta, Brian Heckert, and Malcolm Randall for their ideas and suggestions and for their critical review of the case.

Part VI

Accountability

Introduction

Accumulating evidence suggests a significant misallocation of medical care resources relative to improving the health of the American people. At a time when the nutrition, health, and training of low-income groups are neglected, there are too many hospital beds, too much surgery, too many lab tests, and too many medical specialists practicing in high-income areas. Who is accountable? Who is responsible? What are the consequences to the manager of pursuing organizational accountability?

When patients complain, how is the manager to know whether their complaints are justified? When he knows their complaints *are* justified, what can he do to resolve them satisfactorily? It costs patients in time to complain, and their expectations concerning appropriate remediation may be low. To what extent should the manager make it easier for the patients to complain or help develop and share organizational goals that will limit and focus patient and consumer expectations?

Managers are paid to help the organization attain goals and to obtain a level of resources and productivity necessary for system maintenance. The various stakeholders in health services organizations include trustees, managers, physicians, other professionals, nonprofessionals, patients, and payers. Vendors and volunteers also have a stake in organizational performance. The authors maintain that accountability is limited unless some mutual agreement exists among stakeholders on goals, satisfactory ways to measure goals attainment, and a satisfactory way of altering organizational goals.

The process of goal definition, goal sharing, and goal measuring is a costly one. Conflict among key stakeholders will escalate to the extent that important disagreement is present, affecting or potentially affecting a major shift in resources allocation. In the process of agreeing on goals, certain members of the ruling coalition may exit or attempt to force out other members.

The alternative to formal accountability is mutual adjustment. Rather than establishing goals, interest groups confront each decision on its merits and its effect on them. Should the organization purchase or lease a CT scanner, provide services to the chronically ill, or purchase or lease new computer services? If any significant minority of the ruling coalition objects to a new policy direction, then such a direction will be vetoed until consensus can be achieved. This prevents major mistakes and time wasted on resolving conflict, in reaching agreement on measurement, and in lengthy discussions with various groups concerning whom the organization serves and should serve and about which services to expand, dilute, initiate, or discontinue.

Obviously, if services are being provided satisfactorily, management need not get involved. This is seldom the case, however, because of scarce resources and high patient expectations. If managers do not systematically attempt to ensure quality and adequate service and access, they will not occur. To the extent that managers have such organizational responsibilities and to the extent that physicians and nurses are accountable to a chief executive officer, managers should involve themselves directly with patient care.

Of course, in some health services organizations physicians and nurses are formally accountable for patient care only to their peers and to patients. Often, however, the manager sees something wrong or patients complain to her. The manager can respond directly to certain problems, such as uncleanliness, lack of information systems, or employees in the emergency room who don't speak the language of many patients. Other problems, such as physician or nurse rudeness, malpractice, and lack of regular physician visits to patients, can be referred to departmental chiefs or nursing administration. The manager can communicate with patients by survey or interview to find out how they perceive services and how services can be improved.

As a rule, patients do not wish to get involved with organizational functioning. They want things to run smoothly. Patients expect to be treated equitably compared to other patients. They expect not to be harmed by doctors, nurses, and others. Many feel their time is valuable. Patients want to be relieved of pain. They expect appropriate access to care, and some want explanations of their problems and the treatment options open to them with probable related costs and benefits. Patients wish to be treated with dignity and with respect for their privacy. They wish to pay a fair price. How patients feel about the care they receive varies by factors relating to demographic characteristics, provider characteristics, and services offered.

Managers expect patients to continue using the facility for services, to complain if they feel they are not properly treated, to make decisions about their own healthcare, to expect only the possible from providers (certain illnesses are not curable, sufficient staff are not always available), to respect the rights of other patients and providers, and to respect the facility's equipment and supplies.

These expectations seem reasonable. Why then don't people in health services organizations behave as patients expect, and vice versa? First there is the lack of formal accountability of physicians, for reasons discussed in the section on physician integration. Related is the lack of dependence by some physicians for income on the organization within which they work or on particular patients whom they serve. Also related is the lack of competition among physicians as reflected in the lack of price and service information for consumers. A consumer does not usually consider choice of hospital in choosing a physician, yet the choices are usually confined because most physicians admit primarily, if not almost exclusively, to one hospital. Inpatients do not usually complain because they are not prepared to leave the hospital if dissatisfied and must remain dependent for service on those about whose services they would be complaining. Many persons do not want to make decisions about their care but rather to trust in the physician. When physicians are reimbursed largely on their costs, there is often insufficient incentive to remain efficient. When physicians are paid by the service rather than by the patient, there is an incentive to provide more services rather than to spend more time with each patient. When physicians are paid on salary or by the patient, they have a tendency to see fewer patients. Physicians and patients are human beings, as are managers, and all have their own failings and strengths.

When service breaks down, what options are open to patients and consumers? Patients may take or threaten to take their business elsewhere. They may complain, in the case of a physician, to a department chief, a manager, or a member of the board of trustees. They may form patient organizations (as in chronic care facilities) to advocate for their rights. Patients can sue to recover costs from a provider's malpractice. Patients can lead healthier lives so they are less dependent on the healthcare system; they can raise their tolerance for pain and discomfort. Consumers can control the facility by obtaining positions on governing boards and reporting back to their constituencies. Government regulatory agencies, national accrediting agencies, and large purchasers can represent consumers and patients in holding providers accountable for meeting minimally adequate standards of care.

Managers can undertake marketing studies to find out what patients and consumers like and do not like about the organization's services. Managers can set up special organizational units to advocate for patients, such as patient relations coordinators, patient care committees, or advisory committees. Work can be reorganized so that fewer people provide more services for each patient, as in primary nursing. Organizational routines can be reevaluated periodically in terms of patient outcome or inconvenience as well as provider convenience. Special units or committees can be organized for assuring quality of care. The manager can tour the facility regularly, talk with staff and patients, and observe how services can be improved and made more convenient. The manager can lower the costs of patient complaints by establishing a hotline. The manager can analyze complaints, their resolution, and follow-up, and can talk to complainants personally. The manager can let patients know what they are likely to expect when they come for services and what behavior is expected from them.

To whom is the healthcare organization accountable? How is it accountable? How can its level of performance be ascertained by those who wish to hold it accountable or by those who are concerned with demonstrating that it is accountable? We have referred previously to the various stakeholders or participants who have an interest in the performance of a health services organization. The manager can report regularly to constituent groups as to performance, plans, and problems. Members of such constituencies can be included on policymaking and advisory committees. Management information systems can be developed to gain access to data needed for planning and evaluating services; data would include information on the population served, the population using various services, quantities of service provided, cost of service provided, quality of service provided, and patient satisfaction. Summaries of reports of regulators and accreditors can be shared with participants and stakeholders. Organizational goals and goal performance can be analyzed as can information relating to system maintenance concerns such as trends in turnover, overtime and absenteeism, fundraising, profit and loss, and new capital equipment. The process of decision making itself can be examined and improved either as a process given certain ends, or by including new stakeholders who are affected significantly by policy decisions of the organization or who can affect them. By making itself accountable, the organization incurs substantial costs in terms of time of key trustees and owners, physicians, and managers; monies spent on information systems; and conflicts raised about present and future direction. But the organization may also reap substantial benefits by making plans more acceptable to key stakeholders and therefore more feasible to implement, in gained commitment from key providers of needed services to the organization, and in sharper focusing of the organization's mission so that goals are more easily reached and justified to stakeholders and participants.

The two long cases presented in this section deal with accountability from different perspectives. "A Personal Memorandum on Hospital Experience" provides the patient's point of view, and "Whose Hospital?" provides the manager's point of view. The short cases deal with managerial conflicts of interest and the management of diversity.

Case Questions

Personal Memorandum on Hospital Experience

1. How do you feel about the level of patient care given in this medical center? How do you think the patients feel? the doctors? the managers?
2. What are some of the problems with patient care in the hospital? What are the most important problems that you can do something about?
3. What are the causes of the problems?
4. As the hospital CEO, what would you do if you had received this memorandum?
5. How would you have solved the problems to which the author refers?
6. What organizational factors would constrain implementation of your solutions?
7. How would you overcome these constraints?

Whose Hospital?

1. How do you feel about what happened to Wherry?
2. Do you feel the board was justified in acting as it did?
3. What could Wherry have done or not done to prevent being fired? What could the board have done? What should the medical board have done?
4. Should Wherry have resigned as the board wished him to?
5. Whose hospital is it? What are the consequences for consumers, patients, managers, physicians, and trustees?

Selected Bibliography

Batalden, P. B., J. J. Mohr, E. C. Nelson, S. K. Plume, G. R. Baker, J. H. Watson, P. K. Stoltz, M. E. Splaine, and J. J. Wisniewski. 1997. "Continually Improving the Health and Value of Health Care for a Population of Patients: The Panel Management Process." *Quality Managed Health Care* 5 (3): 41–51.

Cleary, P. D., et al. "Patients Evaluate Their Care: A National Survey." *Health Affairs* 10 (winter 1991): 254–267.

Council on Ethical and Judicial Affairs, American Medical Association. "Ethical Issues in Managed Care." *Journal of the American Medical Association* 273, no. 4 (25 January 1995): 330–336.

Griffith, J. R. *The Moral Challenges of Health Care Management.* Chicago: Health Administration Press, 1993.

Kenagy, J. W., D. M. Berwick, and M. F. Shore. 1999. "Service Quality in Health Care." *Journal of the American Medical Association* 281 (7): 661–5.

Leebov, W., and G. Scott. *Service Quality Improvement: The Customer Satisfaction Strategy for Health Care.* Chicago: American Hospital Publishing, 1993.

Mechanic, D. 1998. "Public Trust and Initiatives for New Health Care Partnerships." *Milbank Memorial Quarterly* 76 (2): 281–302.

Strasser, S., and R. M. Davis. *Measuring Patient Satisfaction for Improved Patient Services.* Chicago: Health Administration Press, 1991.

Case 13

A Personal Memorandum on Hospital Experience

Elias S. Cohen

Recently, I spent some 17 days in a hospital of very fine repute, indeed, one of the finest medical centers of the East. While there I underwent two surgical assaults on my system and had sufficient time to do some observing from a patient's point of view.

I occupied a semiprivate room and enjoyed the company of one roommate during my entire stay. My roommate was a man 72 years of age, in the hospital receiving treatment for metastatic carcinoma of the esophagus. While he had been in this country for some 30 years, his command of the English language was not good; indeed, he was most comfortable speaking in his native German. He was fully ambulatory and received cobalt therapy daily. His esophagus was somewhat obstructed so that it was necessary for him to subsist on a bland and liquid diet.

In contrast to my own situation he was very much alone. His wife had passed away four months earlier. They had been childless. A dog which they had had for 16 years had died about five or six months before his wife passed away. He had a sister in New York, a brother in Florida, and a brother in Australia. His sister visited him once a week, and he received mail at least every other day.

This, then, was the environment in which I resided while recovering from two operations performed a week apart. These observations are in no way meant to suggest that the situations I encountered were the case in all situations, or were necessarily typical throughout this one hospital. I was stimulated, however, by this experience to reflect upon the meaning of hospital care for some patients and the impact of various aspects of hospital operation on the consumer of hospital service.

On Admissions

I had been told that I was to be at the hospital at 10:30 a.m. to be admitted for hospitalization. I arrived shortly before that only to learn that hospital admissions were scheduled for 11:00 a.m. I was asked to have a seat in a very pleasant lounge, and I thereupon waited for about an hour before I was called by an admitting clerk. The admitting clerk took the usual information and received the customary authorizations for treatment, waivers, etc. She was most pleasant and told me that it would probably be some time before the room would be ready. In this case she suggested that I might want to go down to the snack bar and have a cup of coffee and otherwise relax. I took her advice, and about 45 minutes or an hour later my name was called and I was escorted to my room.

Upon arriving at the room I found that the bed was not made, the floor was not swept; indeed, it was visibly dirty. I was told I might want to go up to the lounge and wait, which I did. Subsequently I returned to the room and found the bed had been made. The floor was still dirty. I asked the nurse if I should change into pajamas and was told to do so. At no point did anyone tell me what the routine might be that first day or ask if I had any anxieties about my hospital admission. There appeared to be no awareness of this by anyone on the floor. It would seem to me that there are a number of patients who arrive at their hospital room quite anxious about what is going to happen, perhaps somewhat awed and afraid of this new environment, who could benefit substantially by having a nurse come in, introduce himself, and explain what the general routine for that particular day might be, including the request for specimens, the taking of blood, when the physician would visit, some explanation about meal service, and some offer to explain whatever the patient might not understand. It may be thought that the very nice brochure that the hospital had prepared was sufficient. However, I would venture that the personal contact, and whatever suggestion of reassurance might be offered, would be helpful to many patients.

On Design

I was struck by the severe inadequacies of design in this facility. The room, which had been designed for two beds, as manifested by the two fixtures for piped-in oxygen, the recessed cubicle curtain rods, and the two call bells, was decidedly undersized. I learned this, to my discomfort, upon my return from surgery on two occasions when an inordinate amount of jockeying and bumping of the surgical litter took place to put it next to the bed. To make room for the litter, several pieces of furniture had to be moved: my roommate's bed, my bed, my roommate's bedside table, and one of the two easy chairs in the room. The only pieces of furniture in the room that were *not* moved were the other easy chair and the two bedside cabinets.

Apart from this inconvenience, I would point out that my bed was generally no more than a foot and a half away from my roommate's. The other side of my bed was about three to four feet away from the adjacent wall. My bed was the one located closest to the door. If I, or a guest, were sitting in the easy chair located at the foot of my bed, it was impossible for anyone to pass between without either bumping my bed or asking the individual to move his chair. While the hospital has very liberal visiting hours, it would have been impossible for my roommate and me to have had more than one visitor at a time.

It was equally surprising to find the toilet fixtures in the bathroom without any kind of adjacent hand rails. Indeed, there were no hand rails of any kind in the corridors or any place else that I was able to observe.

These deficiencies in room size and design are all the more surprising when one considers that this building was constructed within the last five years.

The lounge on this floor, which is the only place where a person can go if he wants to walk outside of his room, was located at the extreme end of the floor. Its design and furniture layout were such that it was virtually impossible for two or three people to gather in a knot to talk. It is a large room with some couches and chairs placed around the periphery with a television set at one end. There is nothing there to invite three or four ambulatory patients to sit in a small group, or for a patient who may have a couple of visitors to go to the lounge and sit in a way that the three people might face each other. The lounge is windowless and dimly lit. It seemed, in all respects, a place that would tend to deaden socialization or the opportunity for patients to converse together. Indeed, as some of my comments below will indicate, many things in this hospital seemed to conspire to keep patients very much alone.

For the lonely patient, and particularly the elderly patient who may be facing a terminal illness or an illness that threatens to change his lifestyle, loneliness can be a very destructive force. With increasing numbers of elderly making use of our hospitals, I would venture the suggestion that just as we encourage nursing homes to take into account the social needs of their patients, so we must encourage our hospitals to recognize the social needs of their patients.

On Medical Surveillance

I could not help but be enormously impressed with the medical surveillance extended to me and to my roommate. Our physicians and the residents assigned to us were in to check with us no less than twice a day and more typically three and four times a day. The residents gave every appearance of competence, concern, and conscientious attention. They were alert and were careful to explain what they were about to do, what it was that was going to happen to us, etc. They were ready to answer questions.

I must comment, however, on one instance concerning my roommate. In the course of making the diagnosis of cancer of the esophagus, it was necessary to insert an instrument into his esophagus to secure a sample of tissue. He told me if he had to undergo it again he would prefer to die.

One day when his physician was inquiring about how he was eating and whether the food was adequate and whether he was able to swallow, he complained that he was having difficulty. His physician explained that the cobalt treatments might tend to inflame the esophagus somewhat, cause swelling, and thereby make swallowing a difficult procedure. However, if it became too difficult, the physician went on to explain, it would be a small thing to insert a plastic tube through which he could be fed. It was evident, almost at that moment, that my roommate equated the insertion of this plastic feeding tube with the examination he had undergone earlier. He had no opportunity then and there, and he was not quick enough, because of his language problem, to complain about this possibility. All through that day the man worried himself almost into a great state of anxiety. Finally, in the evening he could bear it no more and he asked the nurse to call a physician. When the physician came, one of the residents, he told the resident that he would not permit the insertion of a plastic tube. The resident said, "I thought you didn't understand it when your doctor told you about it," and he then went on in a very calm, kind, and humane manner to explain to my roommate that this would be a very simple and painless procedure that had no relationship to the examination he had undergone earlier. This came as a great relief to my roommate, but he had spent a day torturing himself over the chance and, indeed, innocent remark of his physician.

The point here is that physicians must take great care, particularly with the elderly, the uninformed, and with those who perhaps have language difficulties, to explain in some detail what it is they might do, how much pain may be involved, how difficult the situation is, etc.

Perhaps the thing that is worse even than pain in a hospital is not knowing. It is the not knowing when something is going to happen, or the not knowing what is going to happen, how much it will hurt, how long it will hurt, what has been done to you, why your body is or isn't reacting in a certain way, what the chances are that things will get better or not get better, how serious some development is, what medication is supposed to do, etc., that is difficult to endure.

On Nursing Service

Perhaps the most noteworthy comment I can make on the nursing service is its variability in the face of extraordinarily conscientious supervision, hard work, dedication, and attentiveness to duty. The level of discipline appeared high—and I use the word discipline in the sense of adherence to routines, safeguarding the issuance and handling of medications, recordkeeping, shift-to-shift reporting on each and every patient, etc.

1. The numbers of staff seemed to be adequate but certainly not excessive.
2. All staff were uniformly pleasant, jovial, and apparently interested.
3. The nursing assistants did their work well and with dispatch.
4. Nurses receiving additional training were very good.

Thus, it is so surprising in retrospect the neglect with which I was treated on my return from surgery the first time. I was brought back from the recovery room about 1:30 p.m. From that time until 9:15 the following morning, with the single exception of responses of nurses to give me painkilling shots, I received no attention from any nurse—

despite the fact that the room was beastly hot and my wife and I had complained about the heat. Because of the heat I was drenched most of the time with perspiration, particularly through the night during which I endured the discomforts of a Foley catheter. Nobody washed my face or offered a cool washcloth, nobody suggested or advised me that I might have a pain shot sooner than I had requested it. Nobody, in fact, even inquired as to whether they could do anything to make me more comfortable. No one came in to straighten a sheet. No one offered to change the position of my legs although it was difficult, if not impossible, for me to move them without some help.

Early in the evening of the day of my first operation, I was visited by a member of my staff who is a registered nurse. In talking with me, she observed that the IV fluid was infiltrating. She brought this to the attention of an orderly, who recognized the situation for what it was immediately, and advised the nurses who subsequently called a physician to reinsert the IV. It appeared this had been infiltrating for some time. Apparently the IV had not been adequately checked.

During that first afternoon and night following surgery I think I had more attention and time from physicians than I did from nurses. On that day and the day or two following, but at no other time during the rest of my 17 days of hospital stay, I found the response to the call button singularly bad. It was not uncommon to wait 20 minutes or more for someone even to come over the enunciator system to ask what it was I wanted. In that first day or two following surgery it was not uncommon to wait an additional 15 minutes or so after I had made my wants known. I think this bothered me most when I asked for some relief from pain. It wasn't the waiting so much as the feeling that perhaps they were insensitive. I am sure that this is not correct. It would have made waiting much easier if someone had answered the enunciator and had said, "It's going to take us ten or fifteen minutes to get to you. We're in the midst of trying to give somebody a treatment," "We're in the midst of preparing our medications," or, "Everybody is out in the rooms trying to serve the patients," or something of that sort. At least I would have known that they were trying, which I am sure they were.

As it turned out, on the second day after surgery I had a chance encounter with the field representative from the State Department of Public Welfare, which supervises and approves the hospital. She was making rounds with a representative from the administrator's office and she encountered me quite by accident. I explained to her what I had found at the hospital and what my experience had been. Following that encounter the nursing service visibly improved. I don't say this to suggest that there was a connection. Frankly, I do not think there was. I don't know what the problem was the first day because as I was better able to get about, I observed the nursing activity on all shifts. They were busy, conscientious, dedicated, and very serious about taking care of medications, checking orders, passing on bits of information to each shift. I can only guess that there is some problem somewhere in the systems review that could make it possible for a post-operative patient not to get some kind of regular checking every hour or two, and some kind of special attention, or at least inquiry, as to well-being and comfort.

One final little note, which perhaps should have some cross-reference to housekeeping. On the Sunday before I was discharged I happened to make use of a urinal during the night. Having partially filled the vessel, I placed it on the floor next to my bedside cabinet. Monday morning I was amused to find the housekeeping service sweep around this partially filled urinal. Members of the nursing staff came and went without paying any attention to this partially filled urinal. On Tuesday morning I observed the same thing with the housekeeping staff, and through Tuesday another three shifts of the nursing service passed over the urinal's presence. On Tuesday evening, a female visitor carefully averted her eyes from this partially filled urinal until I pointed it out to set her somewhat at ease, explaining that I was then in the midst of an experiment. I was discharged from the hospital Thursday morning and at about ten o'clock I confessed to the nurses on duty that I had not said anything to anybody about this partially filled urinal, which had stood there since Sunday night, but that I felt compelled to do so at this juncture since it might conceivably upset any patient who followed me into that room if that urinal was still there. The nurses were visibly upset by this. It was certainly not my intent to upset them and it was not a perverted sense of whimsy that led me to leave the urinal there. It does indicate, however, that there is some confusion about responsibility between the nursing service and the housekeeping service or else the nursing staff is either unobservant or embarrassed. I can't believe either of the latter and must confess being baffled as to how this could occur.

It is, indeed, difficult to understand the variation of level of service among this group of bright, alert, pleasant, and conscientious professionals. Indeed, I would not hesitate to employ any of them to pursue duties in my office or in any institution for which I might have some responsibility. How and why these things can occur is a matter that deserves considerable study. Indeed, it is a matter that requires more study than chastising. My guess is that a look at the work of the nurses would indicate some fault or deficiency with the systems that have been designed for them to follow.

On Food Service

The food service at this hospital had an error incidence of between 20 and 30 percent, which is almost beyond belief. Certainly no less than one in five meals, and more likely one in three meals, was served with either small or great errors. These errors included no meal being served at all despite the fact that no stop had been ordered; dry toast being served my roommate, who was on a very strict liquid diet; failure to include part of my roommate's meal, although his caloric intake was a matter of grave concern to the physicians; minor absurdities such as soup being served to both of us with no spoons on either tray and none available on the floor; the use of a palatized system for keeping hot things hot with a palate omitted from under the plate; or the sending up of a plate with a hot palate under it and nothing on the plate; and on to inappropriate silverware, no silverware, the almost unbelievable use of picnic-type plastic ware for eating, etc.

One obvious difficulty, in my opinion, lay in the nature of the form used for selecting menu items. While this form was adequate for telling the cooks what they had to prepare on the following day (it was a mark sensed form that could be run through an IBM machine to calculate how many portions of each item were necessary), its layout was such that anyone trying to check the trays on a trayveyor system against the form would either go blind or out of his mind after looking at about ten of these.

Another problem, I believe, lay in the inadequate communication between the floor dietitians and the kitchen dietitians. While my own situation was not terribly important so far as diet was concerned, that of my roommate was. He was on a very strict liquid diet. He was losing weight steadily. This was a matter of considerable concern to his physicians. It was not until his physician complained bitterly about the inattention to his patient's food that the dietary service made some sincere attempt to develop foods my roommate might conceivably enjoy. Some of the choices that they gave him can only be described as almost vile. While taste is a personal matter, it is hard to believe that anyone who has ever tasted liver baby food would try to offer this as being a tasty dish. Despite the fact that my roommate had indicated he could not abide a bacon flavor in blended eggs, he was served blended eggs with bacon. I had to protest this kind of neglect and oversight to two dietitians and a physician before I felt any impression had been made in the dietary service.

I cannot believe that an error rate anywhere close to that which the dietary service produced would be tolerated for as long as 24 hours in the hospital's pharmacy or in their central supply, or if operating rooms were inappropriately prepared for scheduled procedures with improper tools, or instruments, available for the surgeon. I would feel that the situation in the dietary service in this hospital is so bad as to represent a virtual crisis because it is so close to almost total breakdown. I have no doubt that there are patients being hurt, and seriously hurt, because of this high error rate. I observed this with my own roommate who, because of errors in one day, suffered a higher weight loss than any other day during the time that I was there. How much of his weight loss was caused by error, lack of imagination, or lack of concern on the part of the staff, is hard to assess, but I am convinced that some of his weight loss must be ascribed to the inadequacies of the dietary service.

On Housekeeping

Perhaps the best and worst that might be said about the housekeeping service, at least so far as my room was concerned, is that it was lack-adaisical and unenthusiastic. I only saw people dry-mopping the room during my stay. At no time was the floor of the bathroom wet-mopped, much less the floor of the room I was in. I did observe walls and the corridors and some other rooms being scrubbed down. This appeared to be on some kind of schedule. However, so far as room cleaning was concerned, it was not much.

I would comment on one other minor point. My room was located just outside the service closet. Housekeeping personnel apparently gathered there at 7:30 in the morning to pick up their supplies preparatory to emptying wastepaper baskets or doing whatever they had to do. They made no effort whatsoever to modulate their voices. The gathering was apparently a noisy, social occasion. They frequently called to each other halfway down the hall and at that hour this was somewhat disturbing.

On Social Services

My experience leads me to believe that, at least in this hospital, a new approach to hospital social services may be called for. It is insufficient to rely on the patient to ask for help from social services. The plain fact of the matter is that most patients are not aware of what a social worker can or can't do for them. On the other hand, a social services department has much to offer many patients who need help from a professional social worker. This is going to become increasingly more the case as older people avail themselves of the benefits of Medicare. Take my roommate, for example. This man was hospitalized for treatment of what he knew might be a fatal illness. He was very much alone despite contacts with some relatives and had recently suffered the loss of his spouse. He was a man who, like one-third of all people 65 and over, spoke with a foreign accent and who might have increasing difficulty with English as tension, stress, and anxiety levels increased.

My roommate said to me one day, "I suppose my whole life will have to change now. I will have to get a nurse or a housekeeper in to live with me. I will have to get somebody to prepare my food. Maybe I won't be able to drive any more." He discussed the provisions of his will with me indicating some anxieties about what his relatives might think about this or that provision. He was not a poor man by any means—indeed, he was quite well-off. He had some plans to go to Florida in the fall and then to Israel in the spring to visit a nephew. He was concerned about approaching his physician about what he could or couldn't do. This man was a bundle of anxieties. Many of these things could have been anticipated from his admission form and by some kind of routine communication from the nurses to the social services department.

However, I doubt that there was any provision for communication except in terms of the most overt kind of cry for help from the patient. My roommate was a man who could have benefited from some effort to find him a chess partner. He had brought a chess board and chess pieces and a chess book with him. This was something that meant a great deal to him. He, unfortunately, in me drew a partner who not only did not know how to play chess but, for whatever reasons, did not want to learn. No volunteer came to play chess, no group workers appeared to help this lone person. I wonder how many others on other floors were as ambulatory as he and who were as alone and as anxious, who put up not only with days and days of worry and anxiety, but perhaps with weeks. When I left the hospital he was completing his third week, and would probably be in the hospital a fourth. His days had very little to fill them after his 15 or 20 minutes of treatment and fewer minutes than that of attention from his physician.

I have one other comment that probably is not relevant to social services but does have something to do with accommodating non-medical, non-nursing patient needs. As noted, my roommate was alone and had very few visitors. Rather than wear the unironed hospital pajamas, he changed during the day into pajamas of his own. However, he had no one to make arrangements for the laundering of these pajamas. He was an extraordinarily meticulous and neat individual and this concerned him. It was only when my wife suggested that she would take the pajamas to the laundry and I would arrange for a friend to pick them up that any provision was made for this at all. It is not sufficient to rely on informal methods for this kind of service. It is also insufficient to expect the inarticulate to call for this kind of service or request it on their own. Hospital staffs must be somewhat more sensitive than they appear to be to these kinds of non-medical, non-nursing service needs.

I believe that social services departments in hospitals must look beyond their traditional concerns and begin to look at these elderly, lonely patients who may be facing a health situation that will introduce major changes in their lives, their relationships, and their lifestyles. Much of this can be picked up in very simple ways. However, the relationship that a social worker enters into will not come easy, as those who work in the field of aging can attest. But the older person is captive and has time, and social service has a great deal to offer in helping him and perhaps his family adjust to altered modes of living, the prospect of death, and of diminished energy and ability.

As a first step, I would urge hospitals to take a hard look at the characteristics of the older people who are coming through their doors, regarding well their length of stay, their marital status, the number of visitors they have, ascertaining on whom they rely, and trying to ferret out what it is that concerns them about their hospitalization.

No one should mistake the purpose of this memorandum. It is not to criticize or complain. I went to this hospital because I sought out a particular surgeon. I secured excellent medical care and, for the most part, excellent nursing care. My goal was to correct a bodily defect through surgical intervention. This goal will have been achieved. Despite what deficiencies may have existed that I have described above, measured in terms of the goal established, one must report success. However, not all cases are that simple and in not all cases are the results so direct. In some cases those good results are achieved only at the cost of a certain amount of anguish and aggravation. Perhaps this memorandum can serve to avoid some of that anguish.

Other cases, however, will not "succeed," and failure may be ascribed to failures in the system. This memorandum is in part addressed to that possibility. Beyond that, I think that all of us have some duty to try to improve on what may already be a reasonably good operation. Here again, this is among my prime purposes in writing all of this down. My main hope is that this memorandum will serve some constructive purpose.

Case 14 | Whose Hospital?

Anthony R. Kovner

Tony DeFalco, a 42-year-old electrical engineer, and president of the board of trustees of Brendan Hospital in Lockhart, East State, wondered what he had done wrong. Why had this happened to him again? What should he do now? The trustees had voted, at first 10 to 6 and then unanimously, to fire Don Wherry, the new chief executive officer. Brendan Hospital had hired Wherry, who had been DeFalco's personal choice from more than 200 candidates, just 18 months before. DeFalco had told the trustees that he shared the burdens of managing Brendan Hospital with Wherry, that there was no way of dissociating Wherry's decisions from his own decisions. So in a way, DeFalco pondered, the board should have fired him, too.

Tony DeFalco had lived in Lockhart all his life, and he loved the town, commuting one-and-a-half hours each day to his office at National Electric. Lockhart was one of the poorest towns in the poorest county in central East State, with a population of about 50,000, of which 30 percent were Italian, 25 percent Puerto Rican, and 10 percent Jewish. The leading industries in town were lumber, auto parts manufacturing, and agriculture.

On June 7, 1979, Joe Black, president of the Brendan Hospital medical staff, had called Tony DeFalco, telling him that some doctors and nurses had met over the weekend and that they were going to hold a mass meeting at the hospital to discuss charges against CEO Wherry. DeFalco had called Wherry immediately in Montreal, Canada, where Wherry was giving a lecture to healthcare administration faculty about the relationship between the chief executive officer and the board of trustees. Wherry was as shocked as DeFalco had been and returned immediately to Lockhart. That night DeFalco and Wherry went to a hospital foundation meeting near where the mass meeting was being held in the hospital cafeteria.

DeFalco and Wherry had been planning the foundation meeting for several months now. It had been scheduled and rescheduled so that all eight of the prominent townspeople could attend. The key reasons behind forming the foundation were to enlist the energies of community leaders in hospital fundraising, thereby freeing the hospital board for more effective policymaking, and to shield hospital donations from the state rate-setting authority. Brendan Hospital had held a successful first annual horse show the previous fall, netting $10,000 and creating goodwill for the hospital, largely through the efforts of DeFalco and two dedicated physicians who owned the stable and dedicated the show and all proceeds to the hospital. Because this was a very important meeting, and because they had not been invited to attend the mass meeting, DeFalco and Wherry decided to attend the foundation meeting. There, they elicited a great deal of verbal support for the foundation, and for DeFalco's leadership. The community leaders were familiar with the problems of employee discontent in their own businesses and with the political maneuverings of former Brendan medical staffs. It would all calm down, no doubt. The wife of the town's leading industrialist said she appreciated DeFalco's frankness in sharing the hospital's problems with them.

But, of course, everything was not yet calm. The mass meeting was held and a petition signed to get rid of Wherry. The petition was signed by half the medical staff and by half the employees as well. A leadership committee of four doctors and nurses demanded Wherry's immediate resignation, and it was rumored that if the board didn't vote Wherry out, the committee wanted the board's resignation as well. Brendan Hospital was being site-visited for JCAHO accreditation that Thursday and Friday. A board meeting was held on Wednesday afternoon, before the site visit. After much discussion, a decision emerged to meet with the staff and employee representatives on the following Monday. The accreditation site visit somehow went smoothly.

The four doctor and nurse representatives met with the board on Monday afternoon, stating that they could not speak for the others. They delivered the petition to DeFalco, who read it to the trustees. The petition stated that the undersigned demanded Wherry's resignation because he was "incompetent, devious, lacked leadership, had shown unprofessional conduct, and had committed negligent acts." The representatives would not discuss the matter at that time. They had been delegated only to deliver the petition. Thus, DeFalco scheduled another board meeting for the following Wednesday afternoon to hear all the charges by all the accusers and to allow Wherry to confront his accusers, 13 days after the mass meeting of June 8.

The meeting of June 22 was attended by eight physicians, 18 registered nurses, five department heads, a laboratory supervisor, one dietary aide, and the medical staff secretary. (For an organization chart of Brendan Hospital see Appendix 14.1) All but one of the 18 hospital trustees were in attendance, including Wherry, who was a member of the board. The meeting was held in the tasteful new boardroom of Brendan Hospital, complete with oak tables and plush burgundy carpeting. The committee's presentation is summarized as follows.

The Accusers' Charges

Perrocchio: The most important thing we have to discuss today is patient care. That's why all of us are here. Many of us are not here because we have a personal gripe, but because we want to do what's best for the patient.

Tully (department head): Mr. Wherry humiliated and intimidated three department heads, Mr. O'Brien, Mrs. Williamson, and Mr. Queen.

Pappas (department head): There is a bad morale problem in the laundry.

Patrocelli (supervisor): Laboratory morale is low. There are too many people in other departments and not enough personnel in our department. Companies who deliver to us have put us on COD.

Fong (department head): Mr. Wherry humiliated Mr. Queen.

Frew: There has been a problem in staffing new areas of the hospital. We were told that these would be adequately staffed. I realize they haven't opened yet.

Tontellino: Several months ago a nursing survey was sent around by Mr. Wherry, and we all sent in our responses. We have received no response from Mr. Wherry about the survey.

Carter (RN): We need more help on the floors.

Greenberg: Insensitivity is the problem. The administrator, as you can see from all the comments made so far, is insensitive to the people who work in the hospital.

Santengelo (medical staff secretary): The director of volunteers' salary should have been explained to the rest of us. Employees should continue to get the $5 and $10 Christmas bonus. It means a lot to many of them. Mr. Wherry has created a whole lot of unnecessary paperwork. I don't feel he heard what we were telling him.

Lafrance (RN): There has been a lack of communication between administration and employees. Mr. Wherry actually has asked people to give him the solution to a problem they presented to him.

Shaw (RN and former director of nursing): Mr. Wherry used four letter words in his office with me. He called one of our attending physicians a . . .

Levari (RN): When there was a bomb scare, Mr. Wherry came to the hospital and stayed for 20 minutes. Then he left before the police came, which I definitely think was wrong.

Leon (RN): It took Mr. Wherry ten months to call a meeting with the head nurses. Problems in nursing have to be solved around here by the nursing department.

Kelly (RN and assistant director): The problem has been lack of communication. I was humiliated when I presented a memo to Mr. Wherry about increases in operating room expenses. He said he couldn't understand what was in the memo, although it was right in front of him. His whole manner was rude.

Phillips (RN and assistant director): When the state inspector came on one of her inspections, she said that Mr. Wherry should be dumped.

Santengelo (medical staff secretary): He told Dr. Burns one thing and me another when we needed extra help in my office.

Bernstein (RN): Mr. Wherry was evasive and showed a lack of concern. He asked me for my suggestions. I told him to put an ad in the paper to get more help, and it was in the next day. Nurses were not present at administrative meetings.

Brown (department head): Mr. Wherry said Dr. Black would also have to sign an x-ray equipment request for $100,000. That is poor leadership.

Ferrari (RN): I didn't like the tone of his response when I called him at home to ask about treating a Jehovah's Witness in the emergency room. When we call Mr. Queen, the associate administrator, we nurses never experience that kind of problem.

Lashof (department head): I felt intimidated by Mr. Wherry. The hospital has a morale problem that interferes with patient care.

Brown (department head): He said to me "If you can't handle the problem" (we were having in x-ray) I'll find someone who can."

Charlotte (RN): I've had a problem with my insurance and the personnel department still hasn't gotten back to me for three weeks now. I am divorced and I have a little girl, and it's really creating a hardship for me. I don't understand why Mr. Gonzales, the personnel director, hasn't gotten back to me. I've called him about it many times.

Lafrance (RN): Mr. Wherry sounded upset and annoyed when I called him at home about the electrical fire in maternity.

Gerew: The problem is communication. Mr. Wherry promised something and he didn't deliver. I have been working here for three years trying to develop a first-class radiology department. How can we cut costs and improve service in the outpatient department? I asked for help from fiscal affairs and I didn't get any.

Lavich: The family no longer has any confidence in its father. There was a unanimous vote of no confidence for Mr. Wherry in my department.

Greenberg: Mr. Wherry has a repressive style. There has been a tremendous turnover of personnel in the nursing department since he became the administrator.

Mendez: There is poor morale at the hospital. The nurses are upset. Mr. Wherry used derogatory language concerning foreign medical graduates. This was in the student administrative resident's report on what to do about the emergency room. Let's remove what is causing the problem.

Black (president of the medical staff): Department heads should be on board committees. No one came around and told department heads that they were appreciated. People at Shop-N-Bag make more money than nurses. Our medical people want to be appreciated, too.

Frew: Tony DeFalco, the board president, is seen as being in Mr. Wherry's pocket. There must be accountability for the situation that arose. I have no personal grievance. Accountability starts at the top.

Black: Dr. Fanchini was behind a good deal of what I was doing. A lot of critical things have happened, making for a crisis situation. Dr. Simba was hired to head up the emergency room, without adequate participation of the medical staff. Dr. Fanchini resigned as a board member. Dr. Burns resigned as president of the medical staff because of his personal problems. Mr. Wherry said that Dr. Severio was not really a cardiologist. The radiologists at Clarksville Hospital asked for emergency privileges. What made the medical staff unhappy was when Mr. Wherry said we weren't going to get a CT scanner and when he said that there were no problems in nursing morale. At the meeting of the medical executive committee held this Monday night, June 20, the committee reaffirmed our lack of support for Mr. Wherry, giving him a vote of no confidence by a vote of ten for the motion, one against, and one abstaining.

Listening to the doctors and nurses, DeFalco felt as if he was a spectator watching a Greek tragedy. The committee representatives left the boardroom. DeFalco remembered when the board had met in the old private dining room only two years before, voting to dismiss the previous administrator of 22 years, Phil Drew, because Drew allegedly hadn't kept up with the times, some doctors said he had sexually harassed several of the nurses, and the hospital wasn't doing well financially. Drew had been a good man, and Tony DeFalco had promised himself that he would do everything in his power to prevent this from happening again.

Wherry's Defense

"First I'd like to go through the state of the hospital, as it was when I got here," Wherry began nervously. And yet DeFalco thought Wherry seemed perfectly assured of himself, confident in the rightness of his cause. That was probably one of the things the doctors held against him—besides, Don had attended Princeton undergraduate and Harvard Business School, and had worked for a government regulatory agency in hospital cost containment before taking the Brendan job.

Wherry: There was bad leadership in the nursing department and in several other departments, a lack of medical staff leadership, and few competent department heads. Nursing is a difficult occupation. Morale is always a problem in this department. These are young people with children; they are working evenings, nights, and weekends; and the work is physically, emotionally, and administratively demanding. The doctors at this hospital are like doctors in other hospitals like Brendan, fearful of anything that threatens to affect their livelihood or freedom. I can understand that. But there is a small, embittered group with axes to grind against me. [For a list of 1978 Brendan Hospital goals and accomplishments, see Appendix 14.2. For 1979 Brendan Hospital goals, see Appendix 14.3]

I have been busy with the finances of the hospital and in improving external relationships with the Hispanics, state officials, and other groups. Mel Queen, the associate administrator, has been busy with the new construction and the move into our new $5 million wing. We've had a new director of nursing on board for five weeks now, and I wish that everyone would have just given her a chance. Dr. Burns' resignation as president of the medical staff didn't help me any, and I have had a director of personnel, Gonzales, with acute personal problems, which has been a problem for me, too. Next, it's quite unusual for someone to have to defend himself on the spot to a list of specific charges that I have been waiting for these past 13 days and just now have been made aware of. I think the way this whole thing has been handled by the doctor and nurse ringleaders is disgraceful. The charges they have made are largely not true and could not be proven even if they were true. Even if the charges are true to a substantial extent, there is still not sufficient reason for your discharging me, certainly not suddenly as they are demanding you to.

The doctors are out to get me because I'm doing the job you've been paying me to do, what I'm evaluated on, and for which I received a very good evaluation and a big raise at the end of last year, presumably because I was doing a good job. (For Wherry's evaluation, see Appendix 14.4; for DeFalco's raise letter, see Appendix 14.5.) Certainly none of you have told me to stop doing what I have been doing to assure quality, contain costs, and improve service. During the past year I gathered information for the medical staff on a new reappointment worksheet so that reappointments aren't made on a rubber stamp process every two years. I pointed out the problems that the low inpatient census in pediatrics would create in retaining the beds in the years to come. I obtained model rules and regulations for the medical staff and shared these with the president, Dr. Black. I questioned the effectiveness of the tissue committee, which hasn't been meeting, and when it has met, whose minutes are perfunctory. I questioned the performance of the audit committee after our delegated status under PSRO was placed in question by a visiting physician, Dr. Lordi. I suggested we explore mandated physician donations to the hospital, as was passed and implemented two years ago by another East State hospital. When patients made complaints about doctors I took these up with the respective chiefs of departments. I investigated the assertion by a lab technician that tests were being reported and not done by the laboratory. I questioned and had to renegotiate remuneration of pathologists and radiologists, all with knowledge of the president of the board, Mr. DeFalco, and I have done nothing without involving the medical executive committee.

I have been involved in the lengthy and frustrating process of getting support from other hospitals for a CT scanner and in justifying financial feasibility of the CT scanner at this hospital. I have suggested ways to recruit needed physicians into Lockhart and have shared with the staff other approaches used by East State hospitals, such as a guaranteed income for the first year. I followed up a trustee's question about the appropriateness of fetal monitoring with the chief of obstetrics and gy-necology, and worked out a satisfactory response to poor ophthalmology coverage in the emergency room with the chief of ophthalmology. I became involved in trying to convince one of our three pathologists not to resign because of a run-in with the chief of pathology. I have to get after physicians who do not indicate final diagnosis or complete their charts on time, because this delays needed cash flow for the hospital. I suggested that the hospital develop a model program for providing day hospital and other care to the elderly and chronically ill, and sought the cooperation of State University in designing a research protocol to measure the need for such services. This action was resented by several members of the staff, although we have not gone ahead with the State research program pending staff approval, or, if they disapprove, I said we would not go ahead with it.

I initiated a study of how we can prevent malpractice at the hospital, conveyed board disapproval of radiology equipment, which we had scheduled to buy but couldn't afford because other radiology equipment broke down in an unforeseen way. There are several very difficult physicians on the medical executive committee who have never gotten along with any administrator or with other physicians. I am the one who has to discuss with the surgeons and the radiologists ways to decrease costs in their units when these costs are way above the state medians and we have to reduce them or face financial penalties.

As far as nursing goes, here is a list of what I have done: I have met with all shifts, with head nurses, with supervisors, and regularly with the director and assistant directors. I hired a new director and fired an old assistant director whom the nurses said showed favoritism, lied to them, and overpromised. This was opposed, by the way, by Dr. Fanchini, former director of obstetrics and gynecology. I hired an expert nursing consultant to help us develop appropriate goals and ways of meeting these goals. I was in the process of obtaining the services of an operations research consultant, at no cost to the hospital, to help us with our scheduling problems. We implemented a study done by an administrative resident on improved staffing and scheduling. I pointed out all the problems of authoritarian leadership, lack of adequate quality assurance programs, and lack of appropriate scheduling and budgeting to the previous nursing director, which is why she had to be demoted. Mrs. Shaw always tried to do her best, but she lacked the proper education and skills. I obtained 15 additional approved nursing positions, including one additional full-time RN in inservice and an additional $80,000 for inservice, from the state rate-setters, something that no one has been able to do at this hospital for the past eight years. Our expenditures in nursing are already above the state median. I obtained a staffing plan from another hospital for the director of nursing and influenced her to distribute a questionnaire to all nurses to better find out their feelings and ideas.

I could go through each of the charges made by the people assembled here, but it won't really prove anything. Yes, I did call a doctor a . . . in my office. Yes, I did leave the hospital after the bomb scare before the police came, but only after I was convinced that it was a scare. I had a meeting to go to in Urban City, and I called one hour later to see that everything was all right. I think it is significant that none of the department heads supposedly humiliated by me showed up at this meeting. You have asked me to resign, but I'm not going to resign. That would not solve the hospital's problems. Firing me will not solve the bad nursing morale here or the doctor distrust. It will show the doctors and nurses and the community who runs this hospital. Is it the board of trustees or some doctors and nurses (the nurses are mainly being used by the doctors)? Whose head will these doctors be asking for the next time they want to get rid of somebody? The bond issue set for next month that could refinance our debt on the new wing will not go through if you fire me. And we shall have a $355,000 payment to make in August which will be difficult to meet.

"Does anybody have any questions?" DeFalco asked the other trustees. There were a few questions, but nothing significant, no major contradictions of anything Wherry had said. A vote was taken to clear Wherry of the charges without rebuttal, and this passed 7 in favor, 5 against, with 4 abstentions. Then the trustees asked Wherry to leave the room and told him that they would make a decision.

That evening, after dinner with his wife and teenagers, DeFalco watched a baseball game on television. He couldn't get his mind off that Wednesday night board meeting, the vote 10 to 6 against Wherry, and the ultimate unanimous vote to dismiss him with two months' severance. During the previous week, DeFalco had made it his business to discuss the Don Wherry situation with the other 16 trustees (Wherry and he made 18). As best as he could recollect, the following was the essence of their comments to him.

Board Comments

Clock (age 55, life insurance salesman, first vice president of the board, former mayor, and DeFalco's long-time confidant): I have been one of Don Wherry's strongest supporters since he got here and before he got here. I was a member of the search committee that selected Don, as you remember. I still like Don personally, really I do, but it has become obvious to me, at least, that Don can no longer manage the hospital. Whether Don is right or wrong, the docs don't like him. (Wherry told DeFalco that Clock sold a lot of life insurance to a lot of doctors.) Don's biggest mistakes have been in not firing Mel Queen, the associate administrator, who never has supported him properly, and Winnie Shaw, the ex-director of nursing whom he should never have kept around and I told him so.

Gotthuld (age 50, second vice president of the hospital board, president of the board of Preston College, and wife of a beer distributor): I have been spending one or two weeks out of every month in Vermont, you know, George, where we bought a distributorship, and last year Sam and I spent six months on a luxury liner trip around the world. So I really don't know what's going on that well. As chairman of the executive committee, we gave Don a good evaluation and if he isn't acting properly as chief executive officer, then at least part of the fault is ours. I see no reason to fire Don abruptly because of these alleged charges.

Lance (age 45, president of a local lumber company, treasurer of the hospital, and chairman of the buildings and grounds committee): I have always been one of Don Wherry's closest friends, although he may not admit it now. I think Don could do an excellent job managing a university hospital, but that he definitely cannot do the job here at Brendan and that we should get rid of him now. Don might care more than anyone else, certainly more than I do, about the welfare of the hospital employees, but Don just hasn't communicated that to them.

Gonce (65 years old, RN, secretary of the hospital, recently returned for the board meeting from University Hospital in Urban City where she was recovering from a heart attack): Tony, you know I fought bitterly against Don Wherry's coming to Brendan in the first place, voted then for Mel Queen, the associate administrator to do the job, and I vote for him now to do a better job than Don Wherry. Don should be working for the government somewhere, not in a small town. Mel Queen will make an excellent administrator of Brendan Hospital. We should have given it to him in the first place.

Giancarlo (age 60, president of a local canning firm, newly elected to the board in January): I don't know much about the facts of the situation, Tony; I like Don Wherry personally, but obviously the doctors and many of the employees are unhappy with him. They must be listened to. It doesn't seem that anything they are complaining about is new or isolated.

Gonzales (age 40, secondary school teacher, was one of Don Wherry's strongest supporters): I see what Don has done to meet with all the Hispanic leaders without any crisis, to hear out our problems and respond to us. Don has reorganized and improved services in the emergency room, hired a Spanish-speaking social work assistant, increased the number of minority supervisors. I am not that impressed, really, by these charges. There's no meat to them. I think this is just a bunch of doctors trying to get rid of Don as they got rid of Mr. Drew, the last CEO, and I do not think the board should bow down to them this time.

Peppino (age 34, senior bank vice president): Knowing Don Wherry as I do, I can understand a lot of the charges and sympathize with those making the complaints. Don Wherry is cold and authoritative, and if he knows so much, maybe that isn't what the job needs anyway. Mel Queen can run the hospital perfectly well, I'm convinced of that. And if the doctors are going to stop admitting patients as they threaten to do, they must feel very strongly about Don Wherry. It's important to calm the doctors down and get on with business as usual, and the sooner the better. Don Wherry will have no problem finding a job somewhere else. Maybe he was going to leave Lockhart anyway after a few more years.

Black (age 45, president of the medical staff): We have to get rid of this guy. He's nothing but trouble. I tried to work with him, but the guys don't like him. Maybe it's because he went to Princeton or something. He gives the guys this feeling that he feels superior to us. He's the big time administrator and we're the lowly doctors. We'd much prefer Mel Queen running the hospital. We don't have to put up with this Wherry guy, and now's the time to get rid of him.

Romano (age 50, president of a lumber company, newly elected to the board in January): I feel the way Lew Giancarlo does. I never thought being elected to this board would involve all these problems, and I'm certainly spending more time on this darn hospital than I would like to be spending. It's a tough thing for this Wherry guy. I like Don personally, but I really think we're going to have more problems with him than without him.

Levine (age 45, attorney, newly elected to the board in January): I think this is disgraceful what we're doing to Don. I don't like the way the whole thing was done, even if Don has made mistakes. You don't treat an employee this way, certainly not the chief executive officer. But I don't think that Don has handled it right, either. He should have gone to the mass meeting and defended himself. He should have organized people to speak on his behalf. That's the advice I would have given Don as a lawyer. And I think it's a darn shame this has to happen. It doesn't have to happen really, if someone would only stand up and fight for Don and his cause. I'm doing the best that I can, but I've only been on the board a short time, and I feel I'm therefore limited in what I can do.

Morrissey (age 47, housewife): Don and his wife Sue are personal friends of mine, but I can't let that get in the way of making the right decision for the hospital. Don is certainly a brilliant guy who cares about people and doesn't want to see the patient or the consumer taken advantage of. He wants to do all the right things and he has done a lot of the right things. The hospital is a safer, warmer, financially more sound place than it was when Don took over. I'm certainly going to vote for Don. I'm sorry, but I don't feel I know enough to be really energetic about this.

Viggiani (age 60, owner of a large real estate firm and chairman of the county Democratic Party): I think it's a terrible thing what they're doing to Don. It's just like with the other guy, Phil Drew. This guy has always been there when we needed him. He works night and day. If anything's the matter, then it must be our fault because this guy has been doing what we've been telling him to do. He hasn't done anything without telling the doctors and us first. I think it's a disgrace.

Asselta (age 70, general practitioner): The staff just doesn't like him. I like Don Wherry. I know he's been trying to do the right thing. I've tried to help Don, after I made sure of him, every way I can. You know my wife has been very sick and I haven't been able to attend to hospital affairs lately as I would like. I guess I'll go along with the majority, either way.

Goldman (age 61, chief of ob-gyn, newly elected to the board in January): I don't think the man knows how to manage the hospital, asking the employees to come up with the solutions to their own problems. That's bad management. Our group is against him.

Catrambone (age 50, director of a large funeral home): Tony, I'm only sorry I won't be at the meeting to speak for Don. There's a right and a wrong, and I can tell the difference. Ask yourself who is right and who is wrong and you've got to vote for Don Wherry. I happen to think he's a pretty fair manager to boot. I wish you would count my vote. Since my open heart surgery, I've got to be in Rochester, Minnesota, for my annual heart examination.

Stuart (age 41, senior vice president of the same bank of which Mrs. Peppino is assistant vice president.) [Don Wherry had told DeFalco that Stuart and Peppino were against him because he gave all the bank business per finance committee recommendation to a competing bank.]:

I don't like Don Wherry. I never have. I served with him on the personnel committee and we were usually in disagreement. Don always made me feel somehow that I was ignorant, that he felt himself superior to me. This is not how he should have acted. And I'm sure a lot of the employees feel the same way about Don that I do.

APPENDIX 14.1
Brendan Hospital Organizations Chart, Board of Trustees

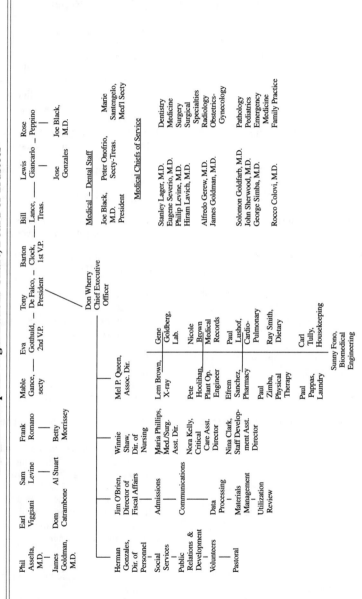

APPENDIX 14.2
Brendan Hospital 1978 Goals and
Accomplishments from 1978 Annual Report

1978 Goals	*1978 Accomplishments*
1. Stablize hospital finances	• $75,000 surplus • Improved Medicaid and Blue Cross reimbursement • Expenditures reduced in line with lower than expected occupancy
2. Increased fundraising	• Modernization fund pledges on target • Successful first annual horse show
3. Improve hospital morale	• Regular employee-administration meetings • Regular publication of *Brendan News*
4. Improve quality of nursing care	• High patient evaluations in survey • New director of nursing recruited
5. Organize department of emergency medicine	• Department organized and Dr. George Simba recruited as chief
6. Establish effective management information and control system	• Implemented auditors' recommendation • Evaluating new data processing alternatives
7. Increase communication with Spanish-speaking community	• Several meetings held with Hispanic leaders • Increased Hispanic staff in patient areas, including social services
8. Increased accountability of medical departments for quality assurance	• Board resolution requiring annual reports • Joint conference committee and trustee seminar for better communication between medical staff and trustees
9. Increased community participation in long-range planning	• Four community members added to long-range planning committee • Wide distribution of annual report with attendance encouraged at annual meeting
10. On schedule, on budget, fully accredited new wing	• New wing scheduled to open in April 1979 • Building is roughly within budget and on schedule

APPENDIX 14.3
1979 Brendan Hospital Goals (from 1978 Annual Report)

1. Stabilize hospital finances and improve cash flow
2. Improve board–administration–medical staff communication
3. Increase hospital involvement of Spanish-speaking community
4. Fill administrative vacancies and recruit needed medical staff
5. Increase pediatric and obstetrical inpatient occupancy
6. Accomplish complete availability of new wing by April and obtain full hospital accreditation
7. Establish quality assurance programs for all professional departments
8. Establish productivity and efficiency goals for all hospital departments
9. Develop an operational long-range plan, including time and dollar estimates for new programs
10. Continue to contain increases in hospital costs

APPENDIX 14.4
Summary of CEO Evaluation (November 25, 1978)

	Self	Avg. Trustee
I. Goal Achievement		
1. Stabilize hospital finance	1	2.7
2. Increase fundraising	3	3.6
3. Improve hospital morale	3	4.9
4. Improve quality of nursing care	1	3.7
5. Organize emergency room department	1	2.9
6. Establish an effective management information and control system	2	2.1
7. Maintain on-schedule, on-budget west wing building program	3	2.3
8. Establish plan for utilization of west wing and integration with total hospital operations	3	2.1
9. Increase communications with the growing Spanish-speaking community	1	3.1
10. Increase accountability of medical departments for quality assurance	1	3.1
11. Prepare to obtain three-year hospital accreditation upon completion of west wing	3	1.9
12. Increase community participation in hospital long-range planning	1	2.2

Rating 1–5 (1 is high, 5 is low)

CEO Remarks:
1. CEO is goal-oriented.

2. He needs to spend yet more time developing consensus and persuading key stakeholders and earning their respect.

Trustee Remarks:
1. Many of these "specifics" are difficult for an outside director to judge.
2. I think CEO's contributions are acceptable except in items 3 and 4, where they should have been significantly greater.
3. Morale is a question.
4. CEO is doing a fine job for Brendan.
5. CEO's capability is great for achieving all goals. Sometimes his motives are not understood, and some obstacles are not of his doing.
6. The answers to some of these questions are based more on perceptions that actual knowledge.

President's Remarks:
I agree that the CEO is goal-oriented. He has attained goals we have given him about as well as anyone could reasonably expect.

II. System Maintenance   2   3.5

CEO Remarks
1. Given what the CEO was hired to do, a certain amount of distrust is inevitable.
2. The CEO tries diligently to establish regular and continuing dialogue with all key hospital groups and individuals.

Trustee Remarks:
1. Greatest weaknesses in this category are in maintaining adequate commitment of employees to organizational goals and developing adequate trust between management and medical staff.
2. The board is not made aware of exactly the number of employees needed and the department that has this need. There seems to be a feeling of unrest among the administrative staff (department heads). Trust between management and medical staff is currently very poor.
3. CEO's capabilities are limitless, but I feel he has developed a schism between himself and the medical staff.
4. Small areas of difference need to be cleared by better communication and understanding of mutual problems. Main problem area is with doctor contracts.
5. I suspect that the only positive factor in the above list would be "maintaining adequate administrative and control systems."

President's Remarks:
1. Our "hospital system" has undoubtedly provided sufficient patient care of adequate quality at reasonable cost. I therefore believe the trustee evaluation to be too low in this area.
2. A mistrust of the administration by the medical staff does exist. I am also apprehensive about the "team play" of the administrative staff. We must address these problems in 1979.

III. Relationships with Important External Publics   1   2.1

CEO Remarks:
The hospital had done well with licensing, regulatory, and reimbursement agencies, and with other provider agencies during 1978. The CEO speaks frequently to consumer organizations and volunteer groups as well and has been well-received.

Trustee Remarks:
1. The CEO had done an especially good job with third-party payers.
2. This is definitely the CEO's strongest area.
3. Excellent record.

President's remarks:
I am pleased with the CEO's accomplishments in this area.

IV. Management Roles

1. Interpersonal	3	3.6
2. Informational	1	2.4
3. Decisional	1	2.8

CEO's Remarks:
The CEO is intelligent and quick. He works long hours and is subject to constant pressures. He cannot possibly talk at length continously with 18 trustees, 40 key doctors, 20 departmant heads, and other key personnel outside the hospital. He must try harder to be cheerful, quiet, friendly, and low-key.

Trustee Remarks:
1. I think the CEO has done a good job in 1978, especially in view of what he walked into.
2. The CEO has weakness in providing motivation, also in recognizing disturbances of uneasiness within the hospital personnel, and in dealing with incompetent or unproductive personnel.
3. The CEO seems to be seeking many changes. His method for achieving this isn't always productive. The CEO has great potential but doesn't seem to implement it well.

4. I'm not too sure if CEO is handling personnel
   adequately. Morale has not improved within the
   hospital.
5. The CEO has done and is doing an outstanding job. I
   am proud to work with him and would give him even
   higher marks if possible.
6. The CEO is excellent on a one-to-one basis. He
   handles groups well. He is anxious to please and to
   get cooperation.

President's Remarks:
1. Changes in staff personnel in 1978 have hampered
   the efficiency and effectiveness of this group. When
   stability of this group occurs, provided the right
   group has been chosen, improvement in hospital
   management will be most evident.
2. The dissemination of information is exceptional.
3. I have confidence in the decisions that are being
   made. I am not sure about their method of
   implementation.

V. President's Summary:
1. Areas of evaluation:
   The CEO has exceeded my expectations. In sum total, I am extremely
   pleased with his accomplishments.
2. Strengths:
   Planning, establishing priorities, dealing with regulatory agencies,
   understanding and articulating hospital organization, financial management,
   intelligence, creativity, ability to negotiate, potential, sincerity, and
   directness.
3. Weakness:
   Impatience and aloofness (coldness).
4. Uncertainties:
   Evaluation of personnel, evaluation of situations, employee motivation, and
   nonpeer and subordinate relationships.
5. Recommendations:
   Attempt to gain trust and respect of medical staff.
   Improve trust and respect of employees in presence of others.
   Refrain from reprimanding employees in presence of others.
   Work toward having assistant responsible for day-to-day operation of
   hospital.
   Continue to attempt to improve morale.
   Improve patience; realize that few people can match intelligence quotient.
   Continue to develop administrative staff.
6. Conslusion:
   The CEO has performed well in 1978. He has acceptably attained his goals.
   As a new manager, he has been severely tested by the board of trustees,
   medical staff, and employees and has withstood their challenge. I believe his
   inherent intelligence will allow him to correct any and all identifiable
   deficiencies.
      The CEO's self-evaluation was extremely accurate. It is comforting to
   know that he has the ability to correctly assess his strengths and weaknesses.

The following elements will be necessary for his continued success:
1. Constructive advice and support by board of trustees.
2. Trust of medical staff.
3. Melding of administrative staff into stable, competent, and qualified team with common objectives.

APPENDIX 14.5
Letter from Tony DeFalco to Don Wherry on January 10, 1979

Personal and Confidential

Mr. Don Wherry   January 10, 1979
Brendan Hospital
Lockhart, East State

Dear Don,

The Board of Trustees of Brendan Hospital, on January 8, 1979 unanimously approved a 10 percent increase in your annual salary along with a $500 increase in automobile allowance for 1979. The above increases will result in a per annum salary of $57,750 and an automobile allowance of $2,300. Your receipt of this letter provides you with the authority to make the stipulated adjustments effective January 1, 1979.

Our board believes that you have done an outstanding job as our chief executive officer and hopes that the above increases have fairly rewarded your effort.

Very truly yours,

Tony DeFalco, President
Brendan Hospital, Board of Trustees

Short Case L | The Conflicted HMO Manager

Anthony R. Kovner

Bill Brown built up University Hospital's HMO over ten years so that now it had 100,000 members, and his boss Jim Edgar decided to sell the insurance part of the business (retaining the medical groups) because University wasn't in the insurance business. Bill was asked to recruit some bidders, one of whom, Liberty National, Jim came to prefer because of its financial strength and excellent reputation. In the process of working with Liberty National, Bill learned that it wanted to hire him, after the sale, to be the president of its regional HMO activities. Bill told Jim what was likely to happen in this regard. The deal was subsequently approved by Bill's board (of the HMO) and by Jim's board (of the hospital). Two years after the sale, Bill works for Liberty and is making $5 million a year, while University is losing $5 million a year. Joe Kelly, University's new CEO, figures out that the contract that Bill Brown negotiated for University was highly favorable to Liberty and now University can't get out of it for another nine years.

Case Questions

1. Did Brown act unethically? If so, how? What should Brown have done? Why didn't he do it?
2. Did Edgar act competently? If not, what should he have done differently? Why didn't he do it?
3. What should the University CEO, Joe Kelly, do now?

Short Case M

The Great Mosaic: Multiculturalism at Seaview Nursing Home

James Castiglione
Anthony R. Kovner

Alice O'Connor is the new director of the Seaview Nursing Home (SNH), a large investor-owned facility in Far West City, which provides services to 98 ethnic groups speaking 68 different languages. Most of the top management jobs at SNH are held by white females. Although Far West City has a 23 percent Latino population, Latinos hold only a 6 percent representation in the higher levels of management at SNH. SNH has an affirmative action program and, as a result, staff members at lower levels come from a wide range of backgrounds. Twelve percent of SNH employees are classified as minorities.

According to Ms. O'Connor's predecessor, Una Light, SNH has had an exemplary affirmative action program, promoting diversity awareness, hiring more minority staff at lower-level positions, and being responsive to the health needs of the minority populations served by the nursing home.

SNH has a diversity awareness training program that has been offered 14 times over the last two years. The need for this program has been assessed through internal surveys and interviews of all staff. The purpose of these meetings is to increase the level of awareness and sensitivity of the staff of SNH as service providers; to promote awareness within the organization and increase the level of informed cross-cultural interactions among staff; and to expose potential problems and keep them from increasing in severity.

Only 8 percent of students who graduated last year from local accredited schools of nursing or healthcare administration were minorities. Latinos accounted for only 3 percent of graduates.

As part of becoming familiar with the organization, Ms. O'Connor has had conversations with each of SNH's middle managers. Anna Gonzales, who is Latino, feels that given the large minority population in the area, SNH is not doing enough to grant power to minority groups. She would like to be considered for the position of deputy director, currently occupied by a 60-year-old white female. Jim Leone, another of the middle managers, points out that white men have not occupied positions of power at SNH for the last 20 years, and that positions should be allocated strictly on the basis of merit.

Case Questions

1. Do you feel that SNH has been doing an adequate job in managing diversity?
2. What, if anything, do you think the new director should do differently?
3. How useful is the concept of "minorities" in managing diversity?

Selected
Bibliography

This bibliography on health services management casebooks is not intended to be exhaustive, but rather a beginning point for those in search of good cases. For sources on the topics about which these cases are written, see our companion book of readings (Kovner and Neuhauser *Health Services Management: A Book of Readings,* 7th edition, Chicago: Health Administration Press, 2000).

I. Casebooks

Billington, G. F. *Cases in Hospital Administration.* New York: School of Public Health and Administrative Medicine, Columbia University, 1959.

Brecher, C. (ed.) *Managing Safety-Net Hospitals.* Chicago: Health Administration Press, 1993.

Coddington, D. C., et al. *Making Integrated Health Care Work: Case Studies.* Englewood, CO: Center for Research in Ambulatory Care Administration, 1996.

Evashwick, C. *Seamless Connections.* Chicago: American Hospital Publishing, Inc. 1997.

Gorey, T. M. *Management Services Organization: Cases and Analysis.* Chicago: Health Administration Press, 1997.

———*Physician-Hospital Organization: Cases and Analysis.* Chicago: Health Administration Press, 1997.

———*Physician Organizations: Cases and Analysis.* Chicago: Health Administration Press, 1997.

Griffith, J. R. *The Moral Challenges of Health Care Management.* Chicago: Health Administration Press, 1993.

———*Designing 21st Century Healthcare: Leadership in Hospitals and Healthcare Systems.* Chicago: Health Administration Press, 1998.

Infeld, D. L., and J. R. Kress. *Cases in Long-Term Management.* Chicago: Health Administration Press, 1989, and vol. 2, 1995.

Kindig, D. A., and A. R. Kovner (eds.) *The Role of the Physician Executive: Cases and Commentary.* Chicago: Health Administration Press, 1992.

Rakich, J. S., B. B. Longest, Jr., and K. Darr. *Managing Health Services Organziations,* 3rd Edition. Baltimore, MD: Health Professions Press, 1992.

Ross, A., and M. Richardson. *Ambulatory Health Care: Case Studies for the Health Services Executive.* Chicago: Health Administration Press, 1996.

Rundall, T. G., D. B. Starkweather, and B. R. Norris. *After Restructuring*. San Francisco: Jossey-Bass, 1998.

Wood, M. M. *Nonprofit Boards and Leadership*. San Francisco: Jossey-Bass, 1996.

II. Bibliographies of Cases

Foundation of the American College of Healthcare Executives. *Case Studies on Health Administration*. The Foundation, One North Franklin Street, Suite 1700, Chicago, IL 60606-3491.

Harvard Business School. *The Directory of Harvard Business School Cases*. Harvard Business School, Customer Services Department, 60 Harvard Way, Boston, MA 02163-9907. www.hbsp.harvard.edu

Kennedy School of Government. *The Directory of the Kennedy School of Government Cases*. Kennedy School, Harvard University, 79 John F. Kennedy Street, Cambridge, MA 02138.

III. On Case Method

Barnes, L. B., Christenson, C. R., with A. J. Hansen. *Teaching and the Case Method*, 3rd Edition. Boston: Harvard Business School, 1994.

Christensen, C. R., et al. (eds.) *Education for Judgment: The Artistry of Discussion Leadership*. Boston: Harvard Business School, 1991.

Towl, A. R. *To Study Administration by Cases*. Boston, MA: Harvard University, Graduate School of Business Administration, 1969.

Index

About the Editors

Anthony R. Kovner, M.P.A., Ph.D., is currently professor of health policy and management at the Robert F. Wagner Graduate School of Public Service, New York University. He has served as senior program consultant to the Robert Wood Johnson Foundation and the W. K. Kellogg Foundation. Dr. Kovner is a member of the board of trustees of Lutheran Medical Center, The Augustana Nursing Home, and Health Plus in Brooklyn, New York. Before joining NYU, he was chief executive officer of the Newcomb Hospital of Vineland, New Jersey, and senior health consultant to the United Auto Workers Union in Detroit, Michigan. He is the author of *A Career Guide for the Health Services Manager*, 3rd Edition, published by Health Administration Press, and of *Healthcare Management in Mind: Eight Careers* (2000), published by Springer.

Duncan Neuhauser, M.H.A., M.B.A., Ph.D., is the Charles Elton Blanchard, M.D., Professor of Health Management, Department of Epidemiology and Biostatistics, Medical School, Case Western Reserve University. He holds secondary professorships in internal medicine, family medicine, and organizational behavior and is the codirector of the Health Systems Management Center at his university. For 15 years he was the editor of *Medical Care*. His other books include *Coming of Age*, 2nd Edition (1994), a 60-year history of the American College of Healthcare Executives, and, with Edward McEachern, M.D., and Linda Headrick, M.D., *Clinical IQ: A Book of Readings* (JCAHO Press, 1996.) He is a member of the Institute of Medicine.